How to Become the Master of Destiny

A Spiritual Journey

How to Become the Master of Destiny

A Spiritual Journey

Acharya Aman

Delhi-110052

© Acharya Aman 2013

First Published 2013

ISBN 10: 81-7386-301-6
ISBN 13: 978-81-7386-301-1

Published by
Books For All
A-6, Nimri Commercial Centre,
Ashok Vihar Phase-IV, Delhi-110052
Phones: 011-27302453, Fax: 011-47061936
e-mail: info@Lppindia.com
url: www.Lppindia.com

Printed at
IIP Printers, D-17, Raja Garden, New Delhi
Phone: 25441120

PRINTED IN INDIA

Contents

Contents

About the Author

Acharya Aman, a spiritually awakened Yogi born in Punjab in Saraswat Brahmin family, on auspicious day Diwali of 1973, is Shastri, Gold Medalist in M.A (Sanskrit with major Indian Philosophy, in which he studied all branches of Indian Philosophy, Yoga, Vedanta, Sankhya, Nyaya, Vaisesaka, Mimamsa as well as Vedas, Upanishdas, Bhagavat-Gita, etc) from Punjab University Chandigarh 1994 as well as an M.B.A in 1999 from Amaravati University.

He spent his time in many spiritual places of India. In Rishikesh, he joined Yoga -Vedanta Course from Sivananda Ashram. He taught Yoga in Yoga Niketan ashram, where he has students from all over the world. Reading ancient scriptures sitting close to Ganges and doing Yoga and meditating near Ganges and swimming in Ganges and meeting many saints coming from all over the India became his daily routine. He had many spiritual experiences there.

Combination of traditional spirituality and modern education, soon he became popular among foreigners and was invited to foreign countries, to spread Vedic wisdom. He travelled and taught in many countries like Canada, Australia, Switzerland, France, Belgium, Germany, and Netherlands etc. His books on Vedic wisdom, his Mantra and courses are changing the life of many foreigners. He has been living in Japan for last 9 years. Now he wants to establish a Yoga and Vedic wisdom centre in India to introduce the ancient Vedic wisdom to modern busy Indians so that each one can understand and achieve 4 purusarthas of life, Dharm, Arth, Kam and Moksh.

Acharya Aman is hope for new era of spirituality in modern India. He can be called a modern Guru for future generations. Look for more information about him at: www.yogajyoti.com/english

What is Destiny?

(Light, Sound and Ideas in the form of God and Destiny)

An insect does not need to go to school to learn how to eat, drink, build a home, find a partner, have children, take care of family, struggle for self-respect and material assets, become old and eventually die. It all happens just with the force of nature. If billions of humans repeat the same story on earth and die in the end, it is not something special. That is why when God's grace starts falling on some soul he starts thinking on questions, such as:

Is there something more beyond this physical world?

Is there any other purpose of life or should I also repeat the same story and die at last?

Modern science can not explain why we are here on this earth, but when someone starts pondering on the complex system of this universe and life, his mind becomes convinced that such a vast programming is not possible by chance. When we look at the world, then this question seems very important to be solved because we see that there are some people who are born into such a family where they have easy access to success, money, love etc. But there are some others who are born in such situations that even their hard work cannot change their situations much. There are some people who are born with some special gift of art and skill but there are some others who do not possess such skills or do not want to learn anything whenever they are given a chance. Some are born to rule and some are born to just follow the rules. We know that there is no soul on the earth who likes to suffer in any way. Then, why on the earth do some souls suffer while others enjoy life right from the beginning of their life? If there is really some cosmic mind(as many saints have been teaching since time immemorial)behind this whole phenomenon, then why is He is doing this? Is there some discrimination in this systematically functioning universe where even the designs of flowers and colors of butterflies have been decided so meticulously or is it something else?

Why is it happening with us?

There are many theories behind this concept. There are many people who believe that Adam and Eve sinned in the heaven of God and all souls were sent (born) on the earth by God because of that sin. But now a big question arises that if Adam and Eve made a mistake, then why do we have to suffer? This is similar to a situation where a court puts you in jail for 20 years for a crime committed by your grandfather or father, whom perhaps you have not even seen or met personally. What you think of this kind of justice? This cannot be called kind justice. Even the justice of a normal judge on earth seems more kind than God's. Then, why all this?

Even if we accept that all souls are sinners because of the sin committed by Adam and Eve and therefore they are sent on earth, then this life for every soul should begin at an equal level on earth. Because when all souls descend from God, they are all the same and they should be given equal chances and opportunities to grow in this life on this earth. That is why all souls should be born into equal level families, have equal level of health, financial status and source of knowledge so that they can learn to do good actions and reach back to God. But, why are some people suffering a lot and some are not?

We cannot believe that God just throws souls from heaven onto earth, no matter which soul is born where and in which family, just as an old man spreads grains for birds in some field, no matter which grain falls in bushes, which one in water and which one in the droppings of birds?

If God is doing like this with all souls without any justified law, it is just like playing dice with this universe. But...

"God does not play dice"

Einstein

And a more complicated question is that if we believe that God has really created Hell to punish bad souls (as many religions teach), then why do some souls suffer worse life on this earth than even Hell with painful diseases or other problems since childhood. Why is God punishing such souls on the earth if God has made a system to punish bad souls in Hell?

Did God change His idea to punish bad souls on the earth, rather than in Hell?

Or is it that God wants to punish bad souls in Hell as well as on earth?

But punishing a soul twice for the same sin does not seem justified because it will not be defended by any earthly or heavenly laws.

If we believe that God is kind (many religions believe so) then why does He need another Hell to punish people when already people are facing worse problems on this earth than even in Hell?

Can God not see Cancer, AIDS and other serious ailments on this earth?

Such types of questions started arising in the minds of ancient Yogis who then started meditating and praying to know the real answers. Through their meditation, the Yogis realized that a very amazing law is working in the subtle layers of this universe and the whole universe is controlled by that law: the "Law of Cause and Effect" or the Law of Karma (Action) and Bhagya (Destiny). As per this Law, the soul continues its journey from one reincarnation to another reincarnation. The Destiny of a soul in next life is determined by its own actions, out of its own free will, in the present and previous lives. God is not a writer of human Destiny. God is not interested making someone sick, depressed or unhappy. God gave all souls full freedom to write their own destiny by themselves, by their own attitude, thoughts and Karma. That is why, it is not God or any Messiah who decides the happiness or unhappiness for a particular soul on the earth, but actually it is the individual Karma (good or bad) of a particular soul that determines his or her destiny.

In the Law of Karma and Destiny, God has not left any scope for discrimination. That is why no matter in which Messiah we believe and to which religion we belong on this earth, we all experience diseases, unhappiness, failures or untimely family deaths depending on our Karma from our past lives. Such problems are faced even by those who do not believe in any God or religion. That is why just believing in a certain religion does not guarantee someone a gateway to heaven after death.

The truth is that the Law of Karma and Destiny is more powerful than any religion on the earth. The Yogis who knew this Law of Karma and Destiny also knew one more thing. They realized that although the soul continues to reincarnate and face good or bad destiny in each reincarnation based on its Karma from past lives, there is a simple key to come out of this cycle of reincarnation. They argued that if we realize "*Who am I*" and know our soul and its direct connection with God then we can come out of this cycle of reincarnation of the soul in the physical body. And, eventually the soul will permanently unite with God. This is called Moksha (Final liberation).

But there were some Yogis who were not only interested in the path of "Who am I" (Enlightenment) directly but also were interested to know how the law of Karma and Destiny functions in this universe and influences human life. What system has God developed to remember the Karma of trillions of beings? Where does Karma live before it affects human life? How does Karma turn into Destiny? In that system, is there any chance to escape or reduce or finish our Karma ? And, if yes, then to what extent?

But all Yogis were not in favour of knowing the detail and teach them to the people because they thought that no one in this physical world can be fully happy and satisfied without reaching "Who Am I ?" (Enlightenment). That is why they thought that only Enlightenment should be taught to humans and nothing else.

But some Yogis thought that there are people who cannot go to the level of understanding "Who Am I ?" immediately but want to live their life happily in this world. Perhaps the knowledge of the Law of Karma and Destiny can make many people aware of their Karma and help them to improve the standard of their life on the earth and turn them into better human beings. Finally, such Yogis knew through meditation that this whole universe is fully conscious and alive, just like an ocean of energy or consciousness. As all drops of an ocean are connected with each other, no matter how far they are from each other, similarly every part of the universe is connected with another part of the universe based on its consciousness. Just as when you throw a stone into still water, it creates ripples which flow very far and those ripples again come back to the same source from where they started, similarly, whatever humans do or think (good or bad) physically and mentally on this earth, creates a subtle vibration in the whole universe and that subtle vibration influences the whole universe and planets and then comes back to the same source (soul), from which it started. When the vibration of our thoughts and actions go to the universe and planets, it is called Karma and when it comes back, it is called Bhagya (Destiny).

Although the influence of Karma comes back to souls from every direction from this universe, the seven planets (Sun-Moon-Mars-Mercury-Jupiter-Venus-Saturn), however, play a very important role in reacting to our Karma, by corresponding with seven Chakras(energy centers) of the human body. These Chakras which are located along our spine rotate like whirlpools in correspondence with the seven planets of the universe in response to our Karma. The name Chakra (wheel) was given to them by yogis based on their function of constant rotation of energy. By taking into consideration the influence of the seven planets on human life, the ancient Yogis named the seven days of the week after the names of these seven planets. Later these names of seven days of the week found their way from India into other cultures of the world.

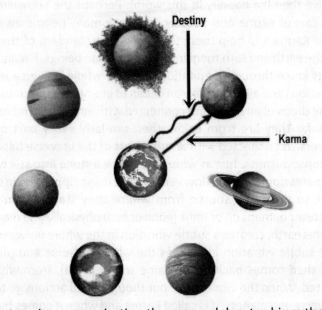

Just as in an organisation the owner delegates his authority and power to his manager and supervisors to run the company, similarly in His cosmic play God has given a part of His consciousness and light to the Sun as a Manager and other planets as supervisors to control the law of Karma and Destiny. The Consciousness which is given to the planets by God is enough to understand the vibrations of our Karma (thoughts or action) and turn it into Destiny.

"Planets are reflections of God which are to bestow results of Karmas of human beings."

"Brihat Parashara Hora Shastra"

Many modern educated people may wonder how lifeless and dead planets can understand the thoughts and attitude of humans and react to them. Please read more details in chapter **"God as Light and Destiny"**

As in a company the President is not concerned with small matters, God has also given such responsibilities to planets under the universal law of Karma and Destiny. If an employee in some company makes a mistake while performing his duty, it is the responsibility of the manager and the supervisors to tackle this issue, and not of the President. God has already created a system of sound justice in this universe. That is why, God does not interfere with this law. That is why it is not God who decides whether someone will have a beautiful, healthy body or rich parents or caring spouse or happy life. Rather, it is decided by the universal law of Karma and Destiny. This is the reason why although billions of people all around the world pray for many things everyday in front of God (for example, for health, money, child etc.), God normally does not answer to most of such prayers. This is so because God is impartial and the Law of Karma and Destiny is active. However, if someone really surrenders 100% of his ego with complete devotion to the universe and there is some good Karma also to help, then only the universe (God) may become active for him and can provide help for something. However, it happens very rarely because the universe is ready to help for enlightenment but for material achievements, God has let the law of Karma and Destiny decide. By establishing this system, God wanted to convey that humans should believe in their own good Karma,and not in Him (God) because good Karma is the cause of good Destiny.

"Age, species, and pleasure and pains are decided by previous Karmas"

Yoga sutra

All vibrations of Karma cannot return and turn into Destiny in one life on this earth because humans continue to do a variety of Karma with many types of attitudes. That is why vibrations of Karma continue to follow humans even in their next lives also. Every bit of Karma done by someone finds its "source" (the person who has done that Karma) at last. As a battery, after giving light to a bulb for sometime runs out of charge, similarly, each vibration of our Karma after turning into Destiny becomes motionless but nothing goes waste.

Planets function like strong cameras all around the Universe to capture all thoughts and actions of all people meticulously. Not one of our movement or thought goes unnoticed by the Universe and Planets. The organism of the universe is so subtle that when even a small needle falls on the ground this is also known and stored in the memory of the universe. The data how many nests have been made by all birds on all trees on this earth and how many eggs have been laid in them in the last millions of years also exists in this universe.

As a satellite knows which vibration should be sent to which cell phone according to its chip or password, planets are also programmed to send the vibration of Destiny to all different individuals based on the data of their individual Karma. As a calf recognizes his own mother out of thousands of cows, similarly everyone's Karma recognizes its "source" out of billions of people on the earth and comes back as Destiny.

Just as a cell phone ,although it moves everywhere on this earth can still remain connected with the satellite, similarly humans can move anywhere on the earth still their Chakras are connected with the Planets of the universe according to their Destiny.

Just as there is a subtle flow of waves between the satellite and cell phones, similarly there is a subtle flow of waves between our Chakras and Planets but we cannot see that. As pictures and sounds move in space before we receive them on our computer through internet, similarly, Destiny moves in the layers of the universe before it influences human Chakras.

You must have heard a story (or you may have experienced) that a person during his sleep has a dream in which he what is going to happen in the life of some person in future, for example an accident or some other natural calamity like an earth quake or an airplane crash. How does it happen? Because those people who had some strong consciousness because of spiritual practice in their past lives or this life, at the time of their sleep (or in meditation), their subconscious mind starts entering into the mind of the universe where the Destiny of each person is moving. And when the mind of that person becomes connected with the frequency of the Destiny of some other person, he can see that that person is going to face this problem. If his mind enters into the "Collective Destiny" of many people in a dream, he can feel some natural calamity also in which many people on the earth are about to die. Because before becoming materialized in physical world, Destiny lives in a certain shape in the universe, which our normal eyes cannot see, as our eyes cannot see picture of the internet in the universe but the picture lives already in the universe in exactly the same shape, the Destiny of each person is flowing in the universe. But from such an example, you can understand that events have already been flowing in the universe all around us and waiting to be materialized on the earth. They do not happen accidentally, as science may be calculating.

As blood flows in our body, the system of Karma and Destiny is also flowing in the body of God (universe). And, to run the law of Karma and Destiny effectively and meticulously, the structure of the human body and the universe has been created exactly in the same way . That is why the universe and the human body do exactly the same things.

The Universe is made of light, sound and five elements (Earth, water, fire, air, and space) and the same is the structure of the human body. That is why, whatever is there in the universe is also present in our body.

Universe   **Human Body**

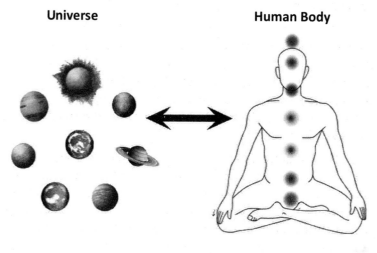

a. Light,   a. Light,

b. Sound,   b. Sound,

c. Five Elements (Earth,   c. Five Elements (Earth,
water, fire, air, space)   water, fire, air, space)

How did God create this amazing system interconnecting the human body and the universe?

At the time of cosmic creation, basic universal Light, which is God Himself, turns into seven other lights (colors) of the universe (Red-Orange-Yellow-Green-Blue-Indigo-Violet) and becomes distributed into seven planets.

" The Seven planets are connected with seven colors of universe."

Kurma Purana

Those seven colors of the planets become connected with the seven colors of seven Chakras of the human body. When human beings open their eyes, they cannot see the seven colors in the Planets or in the universe but they exist everywhere all around us which humans know from the Rainbow. And if human beings close their eyes, they cannot see the seven colors inside their body. But they also exist as seven colors of seven Chakras in the human body (Aura). Inside and outside, our universe and our body are full of colors but we cannot see them. Please see the diagram to understand the whole cosmic creation.

God is not the only universal Light but He is universal sound (Oooo..mmmm) also. That is why, God is known as Nad-Braham (Sound God) also. "Ooo..mmmm" sound and "Bright Milky Light" are the first manifestations of God. But this is not the whole story because God is the mind of the universe also . That is why all ideas come from Him. I will explain about it more in the chapter *"God as Idea and Destiny"*.

As the first universal light turns into seven colors of the universe and is distributed in the planets, similarly the first universal sound (Oooo...mmm) turns into seven other sounds (Silent Om-Am-Ham-Yam-Ram-Vam-Lam) and is distributed into the sound of seven planets. Further, these seven sounds of the planets become connected with the seven sounds of the Chakras in the human body in the same way as the seven colors of the planets and the seven colors of the Chakras of the human body become connected with each other.

It is difficult for people to believe that there is any sound in any planet or inside their own body. But as there are colors in the universe and colors in the Chakras of our body, similarly there are sounds in the planets and seven sounds in the human body. Not only the Indian saints but thinkers from the west like Pythagoras (6th Century Greek Master of mathematics and harmonics), also mentioned about the mysterious Music of the Spheres. He taught that each planet has its own unique sound in the universe.

The seven planets, connected with seven colors and seven sounds of whirlpools of energy chakras in human body rotate the destiny of the all humans (souls) based on their individual past Karma. This is the simple mystery how planets interfere with human destiny. Although light and sound both play an important part in running human destiny, light plays a more important role. That is why a special branch of knowledge was also developed to understand the role of this light (Jyoti) of all planets in human destiny, which was later called Jyotish (Vedic Astrology).

The five elements (Earth, water, fire, air, space) help to create the human body on which the drama of Karma and Destiny is enacted but these five elements depend for their existence and function mainly on Light and Sound.

Good Destiny makes the colors and sounds of the Chakras of the human body strong in a person. Weak destiny makes the colors and sounds of the Chakras of the human body weak for a person. Now some scientists are coming to this conclusion that there is some connection between colors and diseases because before someone starts falling sick, his Aura also starts changing. But science is not very much sure yet how colors can be connected with destiny.

Humans should understand the great ancient secret from ancient Yogis that when light and sound function at the universal level, they can be called God and when they work at an individual level in the Chakras of some individuals, they can be called Destiny.

Good or bad Destiny is actually like a seed in the seven Chakras in the human body and starts sprouting when a soul is born on earth. Those people who have strong Destiny get success, happiness and approach to great ideas. Those people who have weak destiny get failures, physical or mental unhappiness and approach to weak ideas or no Ideas.

Jyotish has been in existence for more than 5000 years without worrying whether people believe in it or not that planets influence Human life. But science has recently crossed that stage of its history when it was even difficult to believe in science that there can be any connection of planets with human mind. Because planets seem to be so far away and how such far off things can be connected with humans on earth and explaining the connection between Destiny and planets to scientists will be a a difficult task. But on a fortunate day, science was able to discover some unbelievable truths about the nearest heavenly body, the Moon. They knew that the Moon influences tides in the oceans. And there is water in our body and in brain also. As water of the oceans is influenced by the Moon, similarly the Moon influences the water of the brain also, which can change many thoughts and ideas in the mind of the humans. That is why some people become romantic and some people cause accidents at the time of the Full moon.

But ancient masters taught that it is not only the moon but other planets also influence human life on earth. The most interesting thing is that saints knew such things in those days when there was no telescope (we know that telescope was invented about 400 years ago) and humans were not able to see the bodies of all planets clearly. The big difference between the knowledge of Jyotish and modern science on planets is that science thinks that the influence of the moon is almost the same for everyone on earth. But Jyotish says that the influence of the moon is different for everyone according to individual Karma. That is why everyone will not cause accidents during the full moon, rather the moon can be highly rewarding for those people who have good Karma from past lives. The Moon can stimulate the brain cells of someone and can give great ideas for success. If someone has very good Karma from past lives, the Moon can help someone to become enlightened also in this life. Many Yogis were enlightened on the night of the Full Moon. Siddhartha (The Buddha) was also enlightened at Full moon. If your Moon is favourable according to your horoscope, meditating for sometime at Full moon night will be very beneficial.

But how to find out which planet is favourable or unfavourable, strong or weak? Ancient saints developed a system, JanamKundli

(Horoscope) which is created based on the time, date and place of birth of someone on this earth to find out the connection between his Chakras and planets, because each person is born on the earth when Karma from his past lives is in mathematical harmony with the present position of the planets of the universe. That is why by studying the position of planets at the time of birth some secrets of destiny can be discovered about someone.

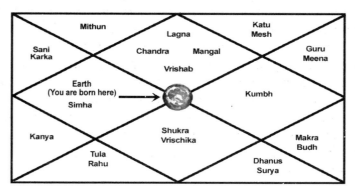

Horoscope

According to Jyotish, all people are born under the special time and place based on their destiny. If two persons have exactly similar Karma, they can be born at the same time, in the same place and even to the same mother. Because of their similarities in their Karma, there is a chance of similarities in their Destiny also. They can go through many similar experiences and can have many similar interests, habits, and passions during their life on the earth. In ancient times, there was no media to know what is happening with the children who are born at the same time and in the same place. But now, we get news that scientists have found some interesting similarities in the life of twin children who were born at the same time, to the same mother but later were brought up even in different places. Twin children like same type of things and sometimes get some physical problems at same time. In some cases they have been found to like the same type of music, cars etc.

But how Jyotish can help to predict something about the destiny of someone? This is possible because there are hidden "predictions" in nature, and if we are able to read them we can predict about the destiny of a person. According to Jyotish, when planets are at some specific position in the universe, some particular events can happen in someone's life. And, these events can be predicted by knowing the position of the stars in the universe. Now, science is also facing interesting facts of "*predictive qualities*" of Nature. We know that for several questions Science has been searching for answers for thousands of years but those answers are already in nature. Science has spent a millions of dollars and years of research to find out how it can diagnose cancer in the human body but the answer is there in nature already. A dog can diagnose cancer just by smelling the body of a person. There are some birds, fishes, flowers and plants which start behaving differently before an earthquake or a natural calamity happens. Similarly Jyotish is saying that particular planets in particular positions can predict what is going to happen in someone's life.

Although Jyotish cannot open all the secrets of human destiny the purpose of this knowledge was to explain about the universal law of Karma and Destiny and advise humans to find a good route for their life and find a final way (Enlightenment) out of this, as soon as possible.

According to Jyotish, basically all planets function together to influence the destiny of individuals, as the seven colors of the rainbow function together from the single ray of the sun. I have mentioned which planet is connected with which Chakra. (See diagram). But in Chakras also they work all together in a unified way. If a certain planet is weak in a person it means (which is known from Horoscope) that certain sound, color and ideas are weak in that Chakra.

Actually to strengthen the weak sound in Chakra, ancient Yogis had recommended Mantra. (More details in chapter **"God as Sound and Destiny"**). To deal with weak colors of Chakras, they recommended coloured lucky stones (More details in the chapter **"God as Light and Destiny"**) And to deal with weak Ideas, they recommended Dhyan. Read more in the chapter **"God as Idea and Destiny"**)

Destiny affects in many unrealizable ways in our Chakras with the influence of the planets. Because when planets influence the Destiny of someone, they do not need to come to earth and give reward or punishment to someone. Planets work from the subtle level of sound and colors of our Chakras from where thoughts are born in our mind.

"The development and progress of the people and the creation are all under the administration and authority of the planets."

Brihat Parashara Hora Shastra

Planets can do many things by creating a little movement in the liquid of our brain by creating vibrations in the sound and colours of our Chakras. Planets churn the energy streams of our Chakras, produce and send a thought to our mind. When we put that thought into action, we have to fall into that situation where we can clear the debt or credit of our good Karma or bad Karma.

That is why to control human destiny planets need only a thought in our brain.

Until people become enlightened in life, they continue to take reincarnation after reincarnation based on Karma and Desires from their previous lives and they continue to learn lessons also of life, in each of such reincarnations. Reincarnation is not needed just to give destiny back for your Karma but it gives a chance to fulfill that desire or work which you did not fulfill in your past life. For example, if someone dies with a strong unfulfilled desire to become a musician in this life, there is a possibility that in the next reincarnation he is going to be born in those circumstances or family where he can start his music work earlier. But along with that, he will continue to face the failure and success based on his Karma (Good or bad) from the past lives towards his journey step-by-step to become a successful or unsuccessful musician. Until the soul is reborn on the earth in some body, the soul (in its subtle body) carries with it the seeds of its destiny but that Destiny cannot affect the soul. Planets and destiny can affect the soul, when the soul is in the body.

It is better if someone understands the law of Karma and Destiny in details whatever ancient Yogis had taught so that one can avoid bad Karma and evolve good Karma. Because even if he does not find enlightenment in this life, at least with his good Karma, in the next life, he can be born as a human being again and can continue his journey to Moksha (Enlightenment) faster.

That is why, until you live on this earth, use your time for spiritual progress and in helping others. Do not try to hurt others. But according to the Law of Karma, if someone is hurt by you without having your intention to hurt them, you should not worry because it is not your Karma. It was their destiny. But if you hurt even a single person with a clear selfish motive, you will face the destiny of that Karma.

If someone planned to hurt someone for his own selfish reasons but could not, still he is responsible for his Karma to some extent because actions are mainly guided by the mind, not by the body. Body is just an instrument to realize our thoughts. That is why, be careful about your thoughts. The law of Karma works from the subtle level of our thoughts also because thoughts also create a vibration in the universe. If you help some needy person or do some holy work on this earth, the universe and the planets store that information. If you cannot help anyone because of your circumstances, but wanted to help, that information is also stored in the universe and you will get rewards for your positive intention.

Sometimes you see a person who is doing wrong in this present life but still enjoying his life now, you may think why it is so. He is enjoying it because some good Karma from his previous lives is still with him. But as soon as the flow of good Karma stops from the universe, he will start facing the result of his negative Karma in this life anytime or in the next life.

Some people doubt and question that if people are suffering because of bad Karma, then why did God not make a system so that humans can remember that for which Karma they are suffering so that people can avoid bad Karma and can do good Karma. But if humans get the result of their Karma immediately within a few minutes or hours, it cannot be called freedom in this universe. Because the cosmic plan of God for His souls is that all souls should feel totally free on this earth, not be under the fear of something like Destiny or God. Because if we want to check the level of peace in some country, we have to see how the citizens behave when they are sure that there is no any police or cameras around them. That is why this universe has been designed in such a way as to make every soul realize that it is free to move with its own choice. That is the reason that sometimes humans think, there is some God in the universe who is controlling everything. Sometimes they think perhaps *life is just a chance* in this universe and no power is looking at them and they are free to do anything. Creating the brain at the verge of these two extremities is the plan of the God because souls are left free to think on this riddle and they are free to decide how they live and choose their actions in this universe.

That is why the system of universe is so mysterious that the soul does not remember that for which Karma the soul is born in the present family and in the present circumstances, because we know that it is difficult to live peacefully in our present life, even if we do not forget things from this present life also. You must have seen some people in emotional disturbances (anger, fear, pain etc) when they talk about or discuss their negative experiences even from their present life. What will be the condition of their mind, if all heart-breaking experiences from their past reincarnations also unfold in their memory such as, when their faithful business partner cheated them in business or wife/husband or child had died and these people are still living in this life with some other family after reincarnation?

Forgetting such old memories and forgetting for which Karma soul suffers bad destiny or from which Karma soul faces bad destiny, helps souls to start a fresh life on the earth in each reincarnation.

When a child is hurt a little, he cries for a few minutes but forgets that experience soon and starts playing again with his toys. Similarly, adults also forget old experiences of past reincarnations and start becoming interested in other things presented to them by life in this life. If a child never forgets a single small experience, how can he move on to experience many other things in life? Similarly, to continue life, humans continue to forget their past experiences soon to taste the next experiences.

But a question also arises that in this situation, how can a soul be interested in good Karma because the soul will not understand that by doing good Karma it will enjoy good destiny and by bad Karma the soul will face bad destiny. To solve this basic problem of goodness and badness, while establishing the law of Karma and Destiny, God gave a very deep-rooted sense of goodness to every soul. That is why, naturally all people like to do good Karma, because this is the nature of the Soul.

Psychologists have come to this conclusion that whenever a movie is shown to criminals, they also want to see the good man (the hero) successful in his efforts at the climax of the movie, not the villain. Why does a criminal think deep in his heart that it is not a good idea for a criminal (the villain) to be successful at the climax? Because even criminals have emotional/love relationship. They also cry for love. Sometimes they do not hesitate to sacrifice their own life for their lovers or friends. Even animals in jungles like to help each other.

There is goodness deeply seated in the heart of every soul. No one is a criminal by birth, The Buddha is residing inside each mind. Although the universe gives the freedom to choose right or wrong, even plants have the natural sense of goodness. But sometimes under the influence of others, for example, when the soul sees that others are doing/achieving something, the soul thinks that it should also do/achieve it. That is why humans should concentrate on good Karma.

We should know also one more point that what we consider as good Karma and bad Karma at some society level, perhaps God evaluates things differently at the universal level. That is why, first of all, humans should be very clear about what is good and bad at the universal level (not just society level), if they want good destiny for their soul, otherwise the definition of good or bad also continues to baffle many people. For example, if someone walks naked in the main market, the police will catch him but from the universal point of view, nakedness is just a natural thing because all species are naked. Even one sect among the Jains monks move about naked. In ancient India, a famous woman philosopher called Gargi used to walk naked, whom even King Janaka used to respect.

And there are many things which are considered normal at the society level but God does not approve them under His universal law of Karma and Destiny. For example, eating meat is also such a habit which has become a common and natural thing in human society along with the habit of smoking and drinking, where the law of Karma prominently plays its role. Because first of all, meat is not natural food for humans, secondly before meat comes to your plate to satisfy your tongue, someone has been subjected to a painful death.

Normally humans think many people on earth eat meat so what is the problem in meat eating ? But we should know that no matter, whether a single person smokes or billions smoke it still affects their lungs. Similarly, no matter, if one person eats meat or millions people eat meat it still crosses the law of Karma and it will surely affect their destiny in this life or in the future reincarnation.

Meat Eating and Your Destiny

To understand the natural plan of God for the food of humans, we can compare our nails, toes and teeth with those of all meat eating animals. All meat eaters are endowed with pointed sharp teeth and pointed nails like lions and tigers to catch and kill their prey. And our teeth and nails are close to vegetarian (herbivorous) animals such as horses, zebras, cows, camels, buffaloes etc. Nails play an important role in catching and killing the prey but humans don't have those. Doctors say even our intestines are suitable for digesting vegetarian food well. God expects humans to be vegetarians.

We know fire was discovered later to cook food and make it digestible in the human body. That is why you can see that meat eating animals catch, tear off, eat and digest their uncooked meat easily but humans cannot catch, tear off, eat and digest meat without cooking. That is why basic food for the humans was uncooked food which is normally fruits, vegetables, nuts etc. Some people argue that they can digest uncooked chicken or fish also. We should remember that our stomach can digest even paper, cow dung and other stuff, but we know that it is not natural human food. That is why vegetarian animals (horses, cows etc.) in the natural environment of the jungle do not eat meat, even if they are hungry and non-vegetarians (lions or tigers etc.) do not eat apple in their natural environment, even if they are hungry because they do not cross the natural laws. But humans have been given the choice to live under natural laws or to cross the natural laws, choose good or bad, choose meat or vegetable on this earth. That is why, the law of Karma and Destiny is only for humans, not for animals because animals are not given this choice, but only humans.

Some humans wrongly believe that humans were non-vegetarians before and had very sharp teeth in the beginning and later became vegetarian because vegetarian food was easily available without risk. First of all, if tigers, lions etc, even though less intelligent than humans, could find their natural food (meat) easily even in all types of adverse situations on this earth and continue to maintain their sharp teeth, meat-eating habit and existence till today, then why did humans (with the keenest intelligence on earth) feel that there is difficulty in finding their natural food (meat) on the earth and they needed to change their food habit ,and lose their sharp teeth or pointed nails ? Another thing is, if nature had really given sharp teeth or sharp nails to humans (as to other meat eating animals, lions, tigers etc) in the beginning, humans needed to keep and maintain those sharp teeth and nails, not just only to get and eat their natural food but to protect themselves from other animals and humans for their survival. We know that humans have always been involved in fighting with other humans and animals on this earth since time immemorial for their own survival. All other weapons, sticks and knives could fall down from their hands any time during the fight, therefore why humans would like to give up their natural weapon (sharp strong teeth and sharp nails which nature gave them) which are always helpful for their survival.

Another thing is, we know that not only humans but also every insect or animal wants food without taking any risk. Then why did tigers, lions etc also not turn into vegetarians, as humans had become, to avail themselves of food easily on the earth? We know that sometimes when they go to attack buffalos, zebras, giraffes etc, they are counter attacked by these animals in self defence and are wounded or lose their organs, as you can see on Animal

Planet or Discovery channel. That is why, scientists also don't know why some animals do not give up their habit of killing and eating other animals, when they can easily live a healthy life by eating fruits, vegetables etc. If scientists think that probably there was difficulty in getting vegetables or grass on earth , that is why, lions, tigers etc had to evolve as non-vegetarians since the beginning (when life started to flourish on earth from the amoeba), then the question is that from where did other animals like cows, elephants, horses, goats, deer etc. get vegetarian food and a healthy life, whom tigers, lions started killing for their food ? Even if you think that struggling, attacking and meat eating were needed among some species during the race for survival and the evolution of life on this earth (which made lions, tigers etc non-vegetarians), then HOW and WHY did cows, zebras, horses, elephants etc remain 100% vegetarians even in this fierce competition of survival for life on our earth ?

Scientists are still confused about how vegetarian and non vegetarian body designs and many mysterious types of all body designs of birds, elephants, zebras, snakes, giraffes, lions, rhinos, tigers, camels, peacocks, etc. originated and evolved from the same source amoeba and co existed on this earth or there is some more mystery behind the whole story of life on our earth. All amazing body designs and life styles of species are not easy to be explored under scientific explanation. Let us take the example of body design of the peacock to understand the cosmic plan behind different designs and systems of bodies of different species. Some scientists believe that to attract a peahen (female peacock) for reproduction, a peacock got the idea to develop his amazing, colorful tail. But other scientists are amused by this stupid theory because they think that the colourful feathers are not the result of the male peacock's struggle for thousands or millions of years (because such tail can take thousands or millions of years according to the theory of evolution) to attract a female because even the females need males for reproduction. The needs of the male peacock and the needs of the female peacock are exactly the same. Then why does the male peacock have to suffer for many years to develop such a tail. We can see that in the human society women also need men, it is not only the work of man to get a woman. The thousands of years the peacock spent in developing a big colorful tail, could have been spent to develop his brain, language like humans for a better life on earth. Because, even without this tail, he could have got a female, as men and many species would have got females without having any such colourful tail. That is why, scientists also don't know yet the mystery of life, design, habits of species on this earth. That is why scientists are still searching the mystery of life and are silent on this matter but some naive scientists are getting the attention of the media by making bigger claims that the mystery of life has been solved that normal people are busy making money and have no time to think about life etc. That is why, people believe in such things.

Ancient Yogis had been telling that species did not choose the designs or organs of their own bodies by their own plan and struggle, even if it is the peacock tail or the vegetarian or non vegetarian body system. A cosmic plan is working behind all body designs, colors, beauty etc of all species. Under that same cosmic plan by the universe, the human body has been designed to be vegetarian and saints recommend to be vegetarians. And those humans who break that law, are trying to put their hands into the fire. That is why, the souls of those people who become directly involved in multiple- animal- killing for their greed will go through very hard experiences in this universe and those who are involved indirectly in this act because of meat eating, will also have to pay for their Karma back to some extent in some future reincarnations by some painful experiences (physical or mental).

You must have seen that a gentleman, who spent his life in peace and did not hurt anyone in society, suddenly finds himself afflicted with some disease like cancer, suffers and dies in hospital at last. Why did this gentleman suffer in this universe made by God? Although someone can be considered a gentleman in human society, his gentleness is questionable under the universal laws. The reason is humans treat other humans with kindness for their own benefits or in fear of some law, not because they are really kind or compassionate.

That is why, if we want to test the kindness of some person, we have to check, what a person chooses and how he behaves when he is sure that by hurting someone he will not get punishment and he is free to hurt or not to hurt or choose to be a compassionate or be a killer. Killing animals and meat -eating etc are also some of those Karmas, by doing so, you don't get any punishment in human society because human society is made by humans only for the humans. That is why rules and laws are also made according to the benefits of humans only. But God calculates kindness based on the universal level, not on that basis which is considered good at the level of human society. That is why, those people who are known as gentlemen according to the definition of human society can be considered as killers under the universal law and can face their dark Destiny someday in future in this universe. If you want to know why universe creates hell for some gentlemen, please watch online some slaughter house videos of those animals which are killed to satisfy the taste of human tongue. After watching those videos, the law of Karma will be easily digestible for your mind.

Science can't understand the cause of human suffering on the earth by using its instruments, because science estimates everything only from one life (single chapter) which is visible but universe functions by keeping the data of Karma of many reincarnations (whole book) of some soul which are invisible. That is why the mystery of this universe remains intact. We should remember that vegetarianism is also taught by the same ancient saints who have discovered universal laws like Reincarnation, Chakras, Sounds of Sanskrit (Read more in **"God as Sound and Destiny"**), Yoga, Ayurveda, Pranayama, Meditation techniques etc even before the advent of modern science. Now modern science is also coming close to the authenticity of all these universal laws.

Meat eating is not a basic instinct like sex. Because if humans don't teach their children not to eat meat, children will normally continue to eat whatever food they consider suitable and natural for them based on their nails, teeth and stomach system. Horses, elephants start eating their natural vegetarian food since their childhood, when they grow up in jungles without any external interference. But if you don't teach a child about sex or teach him against sex, still when he grows up, naturally he knows how to behave in sex. That is why sex was the plan of God for humans, not meat eating. But humans make a big noise regarding sex but they don't criticize meat. That is why, the mind of the society and the mind of the universe are in opposite directions. The law of Karma and Destiny functions at the universal level, and not at the social level, which humans have created by themselves.

It was not only the Indian saints who were vegetarians but many thinkers from the western world like Einstein, Thomas Edison, Newton, Plato, Socrates, Aristotle, Immanuel Kant, Pythagoras, Abraham Lincoln and others reached this conclusion slowly that humans are created vegetarian in this cosmic plan and have turned into vegetarians even in that western society where meat eating had been a common culture.

Milk and dairy products are also from animals but ancient saints were liberal to use such products because to get milk you don't have to give pain or kill animals. But saints also recommended if you want to take the milk of animals, give them due respect in return. Humans can make many uses of animals also if they do so without hurting or killing them.

If you eat meat for health and power, you should feel sorry for your ignorance because you can see with your own eyes that vegetarian animals like horses, elephants, zebras, bulls, rhinos etc are strong, energetic, bigger and healthy with their vegetarian diet and they have never tasted meat in their life. And these animals even don't read books on nutrition or proteins, as humans study in human society. But by big advertisements, humans have been forced to believe that they will have deficiency in their body if they depend on vegetarian diet. Symbolizing the power of car engine as Horse Power (HP), not lion power is also an example of the long lasting power, stamina and patience which a vegetarian animal horse possesses. Vegetarian food gives more stamina and energy but meat eating increases impatience, wildness, anger and body-weight in humans. Because of increasing impatience and wildness among humans, relationships are breaking quickly. Because when natural habits (like food) are changed into some kind of negative habit, some kind of bad reaction is possible from nature. For example, as I have mentioned earlier that cows are created naturally vegetarians but if you start giving them unnatural food, there can be problems. *"Mad Cow Disease"* happened because some people started feeding them with beef and meat particles by thinking that for survival animals can eat anything. Food is just food, meat or vegetabales. And meat started showing negative results on the body and mind of cows and cows became mad. Similarly, human consciousness has been changing dangerously because of eating unnatural food (meat) which will take the planet earth towards psychological disorders, broken relationships , wars and other problems.

The Law of Karma is against non-vegetarian humans, not only just because they destroy some animals or birds to satisfy their tongue but it works because they crush the love also in some. Because when fruit and tree are separated from each other, there is no layer of love between that fruit and the tree but all animals and birds are connected with their children and family with a strong feeling of love, as humans are. Birds and animals want to produce their children where they feel, they are safe, as humans like to do. If we walk under the nest of some birds , they would not like to throw their eggs to be eaten by humans as trees throw their fruits to the ground , but their droppings on our head (as many crows do) to protect their home and young ones.

And when some bird or animal is killed, the innocent feeling of love is also killed at that time. And anyone who is responsible for killing someone's body and love, can't get love or live peacefully in this universe. This is the simple law of Karma and Destiny.

Thomas Edison said:

"Non-violence leads to the highest ethics, which is the goal of all evolution. Until we stop harming all other living beings, we are still savages."

As animals balance nature by eating their respective food, similarly by eating fruits and vegetables, humans can help the ecology. Because when humans, animals and birds eat fruits and vegetables, nature and trees again continues to grow and spread from seeds which they throw after eating the pulp or when seeds pass through their excreta. But when you kill an animal, you not only kill a feeling of love but you kill the flow of life also, which is important for chain work of nature.

"Nothing will benefit human health and increase chances for survival of life on Earth as much as the evolution to a vegetarian diet."

Einstein

Some people tell me that although fruit and trees don't have love-feeling as birds, animals and humans have but there is consciousness and life in fruits, trees and plants also. If we eat fruit and vegetables, still we hurt them. If God is worried about pain, then why did God not create something totally "lifeless" for our food? The simple answer is, God can't do it because God has His own mathematical limitations. He has created the universe mathematically, as we know from the millions of geometrical designs of flowers and butterflies in our world. He does not go out of that. God can't make a triangle with two lines. Similarly, He can't make anything in this universe which is totally unconscious. Because God is everywhere and every part of this universe is conscious. It is useless if some fish complains to the ocean why there is wetness everywhere in ocean. This whole universe is like an ocean. We are living in God. In and out, there is consciousness. If God takes out His consciousness from behind this universe, how can this life cycle exist ? That is why; nothing can be unconscious here in this universe, even though something can seem unconscious. Even the lowest ladder of consciousness Atom, which God created, is also conscious. If atoms are also 100% unconscious, everything in this universe will fall apart. Consciousness is necessary to connect everything with every other thing in this universe. Even the law of Karma also runs because of the consciousness of planets and space.

Although there is consciousness in atoms, plants and vegetables, but in animals and birds, it has grown to LOVE level. That is why; birds and animals also fall in love as humans do. In many cases, they are better lovers and more faithful than humans. There are some birds, for example, cranes; the love between this pair is so strong that if one dies, the other also will die naturally in pain of separation. Pigeons have such a great sensitivity that they can find their owner and come back home even from a distance of thousands of kilometers. Many species have some kind of talent which even humans can feel jealous of.

How many animals and birds kill their parents in jungles for their selfish reasons? But it happens in the human society. That is why birds and animals also need to be respected. If all species are just a food for humans or they don't have souls, then why are they sensitive about their families more than even humans?

Actually the souls of all insects, birds, animals are also on the ladder of evolution just like the souls of humans. Under the universal plan of God, they are not just our food or they are not to be treated in whatsoever way as humans like.

After creating thousands of wars of hate and killing and maiming billions of innocent men, women and children in those wars and making millions of people slaves on this earth, still humans have been thinking that they are civilized and kind but animals are beasts and dangerous or just a food. You can see that although on the one hand humans and countries talk about equality and harmony on this earth but on the other hand, they are trying to overpower others and want to be superior to others. It was happening thousands of years ago also and it is happening even today and it will happen in the future also. That is why more money has been spent on weapons and war preparations in the last hundred years on this earth rather than on urgent basic necessities of human life as food, education, medicine etc. This is the hard truth of human values on earth. Humans can make any definition for themselves and make any definitions for other creatures of the earth. That is why the Law of Karma is active in this universe to put things in a proper way.

Please don't think that if something is accepted by millions of humans on earth, perhaps God can also change His way of judgment, whether it is meat eating or something else. Humans should be clear that earth and humans are not the highest priority for God because God has many other worlds to take care of in the universe. That is why God never changes His universal laws.

God did not create humans to see how much technologically or financially they advance. God does not mind even if we don't make any temples or churches etc for Him. God does not live in heaven or temples or churches. Because at the time of natural calamities all spiritual buildings are also destroyed. God is in the universe and nature everywhere. When we are grateful to nature and the laws of nature, we are grateful to God. God's ways are just. That is why, those people who don't believe in God but are vegetarians will have more good destiny after death than those people, who believe in God but eat meat.

Does "Meat eating" or "Violence" always create Bad Destiny?

There are more secrets about the law of Karma, and without knowing them the knowledge of Karma will not be complete. Actually "intention" and "desire" behind some actions determine the result of our Karma, not just physical action (such as meat eating or violence). Under this rule "exactly the same Karma" done by two different people with different intention or desire creates different results. It means that meat eating and violence can bring bad destiny for some people, but not for some.

How does this law work ?

Please take an example to understand it. A man enters a school playground where hundreds of children are playing, and starts killing children one by one with a knife. A woman teacher, who is present there at that time wants to stop him physically but she can not. If she calls the police for help, it may be too late. Because until then, all children will be killed. She has a gun in the office for security but she is confused whether she should use it or not. But she goes to the office and brings the gun and shoots the man. Because not stopping that man means losing the lives of hundreds of children.

What religions and the messiahs say about such situations because she killed a person? Is it violence? What about her Karma of killing that person? The Karma of that woman will not bring bad Destiny. The woman is not killing the person to satisfy her own desire. Because according to the Law of Karma described in the Bhagvat Gita (Divine Song) by Krishna, if someone enters into some action without having the intention to satisfy his own selfish desire, greed or taste that Karma can't bring bad destiny. That is why the Gita recommends that believing in only that "non-violence" is good for humans which increases peace in society, not in that "non-violence" which increases violence. Because just saying "Don't kill" will not be enough to describe good or bad.

That is why, in the law of Karma, sometimes violence (if not misunderstood and not done with selfish motives) can be a good Karma and on the other hand, sometimes helping (which is given with hidden desire to exploit someone in future) can be bad Karma.

Sometimes soldiers participate in war or sometimes many creatures are killed during farming and agriculture by a farmer, but both are not responsible for their Karma. Because it is not their personal desire to kill. They are just doing their duty under available circumstances. But those people who start war for their selfish reasons will pay for their Karma. Similarly, those people, who live in those islands, where they don't have any other choice regarding food except meat, can be free from their Karma. But those humans who have CHOICE of food, vegetarian or meat, but are still choosing meat to satisfy personal choice or taste, will pay for their Karma someday somehow in this universe. Because where there is a choice ,there is destiny. Where there is no choice, there is no destiny.

Normally people want to get results of their good Karma and want to avoid the results of their bad Karma. But in the law of Karma, there is no discrimination. If you don't want the results of your bad action in this universe, first you have to learn how to do good actions also without expecting good results/returns/appreciation from it. But just as humans can't give up their desires to get results for their good Karma, similarly the universe also can not refrain from giving the results of their bad Karma also. An enlightened person lives his life without expecting the results of his good Karma from the humans or the universe, which is why; he is free from the results of all Karma (good or bad) in this universe. For example just as a slap on your face from a small one year old kid does not make you angry and a slap on your face from your rival creates anger in your mind, similarly, any action done by some enlightened person and action done by other people, vibrates the universe differently. The reason is that the attitude of an enlightened person and the attitude of a normal person are totally different and are understood by the universe very well. That is why, if the Buddha, Krishna, Jesus or any other enlightened person eats meat or creates violence on this earth, he will remain untouched by the universal law of Karma and Destiny, but if you choose to kill even a sparrow or choose to eat meat, your soul cannot remain untouched by the universal law of Karma and Destiny.

If you want to protect yourself from bad destiny, you are left with 3 options now:

1. be enlightened first

2. give up meat or very bad karma first, or

3. give up the desire to get the results of your good Karma first (because then bad Karmas also don't affect you)

We should know that the laws of some countries are not made to put someone in jail for his bad actions, but to make him realize that he must not repeat the same thing again. But where is the guarantee that he will not repeat the mistake or crime, although he can promise in front of the magistrate of justice not to repeat it ? Because the police and the magistrate can't read the mind of a criminal. That is why; the earthly laws are made in such a way, as to put a criminal in jail for a long time to make him realize his mistake. But if in future, science develops a device to read the mind of a criminal and finds that a certain thief or robber or killer has become a totally changed person at heart and will never repeat his action, then most probably the punishment can be less severe. Because such a person is not a problem anymore in the society and there is no question of putting him in jail now, instead he can be more useful to the society to teach people with the experiences of his personal mistakes. But the universal law of Karma and destiny is more advanced and kinder than the police and the magistrate on this earth because it recognizes even our thoughts. Normally our earthly laws work with evidences. If evidences are against you, you will go to jail. But evidences can be wrong also. That is why earthly laws sometimes work blindly and that is why, the law of the universe, goes with our thoughts and attitude. Because thoughts and attitude can never be mistaken. They are with us always. We can just look into ourselves and see what we are. The Universe is also looking into us. That is why if someone speaks to the universe from his heart not to repeat some wrong action again, which he has been repeating all his life, the universe and the Planets can read his thoughts and destiny becomes less aggressive for him. As you know that on our earth when some criminal shows good behavior during his jail term his punishment becomes less for him. That is why, you should promise to the universe from heart what bad Karma you are not going to repeat.

You must have realized by now that what is good or bad at the universal level and what things you should do for the better journey of your soul in this universe.

By the Grace of God I have tried to put the entire law of Destiny in a simple language which is taught by ancient Yogis more than 5000 years ago. But if still any confusion arises in your mind about what is good Karma or Bad Karma, then remember one thing that only those Karmas are good which you expect from others for yourself and only those Karmas are bad which you do not expect from others for yourself. The Universe judges our Karma as we judge the actions of others towards us. Under this rule, if we do not like to suffer pain caused by other humans or animals, we should also never give pain to humans and animals. But if you think that your family is family and your pain is pain but animals' and other humans' family is no family and their pain is no pain, be very careful about this attitude.

The Universe keeps this secret from humans about which part of their life is influenced by Destiny and which part of life is influenced because of their own mistakes or Karma in this present life. That is why humans should not give up hope to do good in life and to succeed. Because this is the only thing that humans have in their hands. All humans are masters of their Karma but are slaves to their Destiny. That is why you should decide your actions (Karma) carefully. Most importantly, decide your thoughts carefully first. Because thoughts push your speech and actions out which create the drama of your Destiny later.

God as Light and Destiny

Until a long time ago, scientists had been thinking that only humans and animals have consciousness and other phenomena are lifeless in this universe. However, recently they were face-to-face with some shocking evidences that plants also have their own emotions and feelings. Plants also like and dislike things as we humans do. If they are exposed to good classical music, they flourish and grow more healthy and if you play heavy metal music or rock music close to them, they wilt and sometimes die.

But there was another discovery made by a Japanese gentleman, Dr Masaru Emoto, which reveals another mysterious side of this universe. Dr Masaru Emoto proved, through many scientific experiments, that water is not a dead element, as normally believed by people. He proved that water also has consciousness and it can be influenced by our positive and negative words. If you repeat respectful or loving words to water, for example, "I love you" or "Thank you" water expresses its reaction by turning into beautifully shaped crystals. If we speak negative words to water, it reacts by turning into ugly crystals.

His discovery also advises us to be careful about the influence of our own good or bad thoughts on ourselves because our body is also full of water which can be influenced by our thoughts. We know that 70% of the earth is water and surely it can be influenced by the words and thoughts of billions of humans living on the earth.

As humans begin to understand the deeper truths about this universe, many amazing and unbelievable things are waiting to be unveiled in nature. We do not know what next mysterious universal truth is going to be revealed by the science of tomorrow. If we go deeper into the Vedic literature (the most ancient literature available on the earth) of ancient India, we will find that the ancient saints, through their meditation, were able to realize every CONSCIOUS phenomenon which has been working at the subtle level of this universe. They realized that all natural phenomena, such as Agni (Fire), Vayu or Pawan (Air),Prithvi (Earth), Jal (Water) and Grahas (Planets), are full of consciousness. That is why these saints developed prayers not only for water but also for Fire, Air, Earth and Planets. Most parts of the Vedas are full of prayers to Nature.

I got a chance to visit Kyoto, Japan a few times, (a world famous cultural and historical centre of Japan) for my seminars. There are many statues of Nature Gods in the traditional temples of Japan. Their origin is also from the Vedas and came to Kyoto along with the knowledge of Buddhism.

Water was respected very much in ancient India. The river Ganges is a good example of this. For thousands of years trillions of people from all generations have been offering prayers to the Ganges. Even today many spiritual masters like to do meditation or spiritual practices close to the Ganges. The water of the Ganges has also become charged with spiritual energy because many spiritual masters meditated on the banks of the Ganges or by standing in its water. That is why many people who want a short cut to spiritual progress, run to the Ganges.

In ancient literatures, there are many references that if someone picks even a fruit from a tree, he should say thanks to the tree or if someone drinks water from a river, he should say thanks to that river, because humans cannot live a good life without giving respect to Nature gods. That is why the concept of "Nature gods" became common in the ancient culture of India.

When foreigners or aggressors invaded India, they could not grasp the concept of "Nature Gods" and they announced to the world that Indians worship many Gods and that they practise a pagan religion. Many attempts were also made to convert the faith of the people of India because they saw people offering prayers everywhere, to water, to fire, to the sun, to the moon, to trees. Even the views of ancient Indians about "Supreme God" in Hinduism were not properly understood by the people from other cultures because the ancient Indians gave many different names to the same God based on His functions in this universe.

They explained that Brahm (God) is the cause of this Brahamand (universe) and He performs three different functions for His universe: Creation, Maintenance and Destruction. When He creates this universe, He is called Brahma and when He maintains the universe, He is called Vishnu and when He destroys the universe, He is called Shiva. Brahma, Vishnu and Shiva are the three different aspects of the same Supreme Reality according to the three required cosmic functions.

As we know that normally if we want to create something special, we should have a deep knowledge and if we want to maintain or continue something, we need wealth and if we want to destroy something, we need power. That is why the power which God uses at the time of the creation of this universe, it is called Saraswati (wisdom), the power which God uses to maintain this universe, is called Laxmi (wealth), and the power which God uses to destroy this universe, is called Shakti (Power).That is why, the ancient Indians kept this trinity in pairs.

Braham

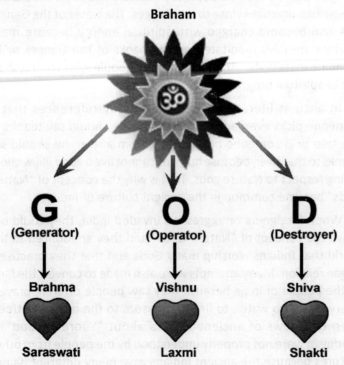

G	O	D
(Generator)	(Operator)	(Destroyer)
↓	↓	↓
Brahma	Vishnu	Shiva
Saraswati	Laxmi	Shakti

Some masters suggested that instead of saying *"God, give me Knowledge"*, you can call Goddess Saraswati. It became a tradition in India to pray to Saraswati in Gurukuls or schools.

And the reason to equip God with "female" powers was to tell the world that as God is incomplete without a female (power), as sun is incomplete without the moon, similarly man is incomplete without woman in human society. People could understand that God is not just "He", God can be "She" also. For many people, this kind of concept of God was difficult to understand. And, it was even more difficult to understand why in the Vedas, there is prayer for Fire, Water, Moon, Sun etc.

After reaching a higher state of their consciousness during meditation, Yogis realized that all these conscious Natural phenomena also understand human attitude. That is why it is important for humans to respect Nature Gods in order to live a harmonious life on this earth with nature because the human body is also made of five Nature-gods, Earth, Water, Fire, Air and Space. And, the existence and function of each visible and invisible natural phenomenon is to make life better on earth according to the universal plan. Respecting only the Supreme God is not a perfect idea. Nature should also be respected because humans live in the lap of Mother Nature and Father (God) is invisible.

As in our human society, a husband has to maintain good communication with the wife more than with his children to run all required family functions smoothly. Similarly, God also has deeper and subtle communication with Nature rather than with His children (humans and other species) to run all the required functions of the universe effectively. That is why, one side of Nature (Mother) is connected with God (Father) and the other side of Mother Nature is connected with us (the children).

By giving some part of His consciousness to Nature (Earth, Water, Fire, Air and Space) God makes His universal functions easier. Even while operating the law of Karma, God operates by giving His consciousness to stars. The consciousness of all natural phenomena understands very well what humans are doing on the earth. On the one hand Nature helps the humans on earth and at the same time it keenly observes the behavior of humans. When things become uncontrollable on the earth and there is growing disrespect for mother nature, the chances of survival of humanity on the earth become doubtful.

The issue of 'how long some civilizations continue on this earth' is not solely decided by God but it is decided by Nature also. When the situation becomes unbearable for Nature gods, then God gives a free choice to all natural phenomena to react in any free way in response to the actions of the humans. After getting a free choice from God, nature starts behaving wildly with humans on earth, as humans were behaving with nature before. Not only the Indian sages but also western philosophers have similar ideas.

"Nature does nothing uselessly".

Aristotle

If God always maintains communication with natural phenomena, then we can reach one more conclusion that first communication in this universe must have happened between the Sun and God because the Sun is the oldest in our universe. The Sun helps to continue the functions of our universe and is responsible also to continue life on earth and he is the manager to control the realm of Karma and Destiny with his seven colors. There may be many spiritual references about it in the ancient books of the world. Let us see one of them.

"I taught mystery of Yoga to Sun first in the history of the universe".

Krishna in the "Bhagavat- Gita"

This quote also indicates that some kind of subtle communication happened between Krishna and the Sun. Actually Lord Krishna taught "Karm-Yoga" first to the Sun in our universe. There are many branches of Yoga mentioned in ancient books.

Karm-Yoga means *when someone does his Karma (duty=action) without expecting the fruit from his action for his own satisfaction, this is called Karma Yoga. What Mahatma Gandhi has done for the welfare of the people without expecting any fruit from the people is also known as "Karm-Yoga".*

The Sun also gives light to the universe to help life on earth but still does not ask for any return for his action from God or humans. All other nature gods- water, fire, air, earth - are also doing Karma-Yoga by helping life on earth. That is why they are respected as Nature gods.

From this statement of Krishna, it is very simple to understand that if there was no consciousness in planets and no subtle communication between the spiritual world and natural phenomena, all functions of the entire universe can never be performed in such a wonderful and organized way.

It is not just the communication between the Sun and God only but there are signs of communication between the sun and humans (who have a higher consciousness) too. Even the famous book on astronomy "Surya Siddhanta" is also a communication between the Sun and Mayasura.

The Japanese scholar Dr Masaru Emoto knew from some of his experiments on water that if water is exposed to specific types of words for a long time, the consciousness of water starts giving favorable response, similarly, the Indian spiritual masters also knew the mystery that the consciousness of each planet can be aroused by specific thankful words. If someone's particular planet or planets are weak according to Jyotish, it means the light of certain planet is weak in the Chakra of someone. If we send a message of love to that certain planet with a grateful heart, then favorable results can be produced for someone's destiny.

If we refer to the ancient scriptures of India, they specify which Mantra is for which planet . I am giving below the easiest Mantra for each planet which can be chanted for a certain planet:

Sun	Om Suryaye Nama
Moon	Om Somaye Nama
Mars	Om Mangalaye Nama
Mercury	Om Budhaye Nama
Jupiter	Om Gurve Nama
Venus	Om Shukraye Nama

Saturn   Om Shanicharaye Nama

Two subsidiary Shadow planets...

Rahu   Om Rahve Nama

Ketu   Om Ketve Nama

Out of these seven main planets, the Sun and the Moon have been considered more important. Because the Sun is the centre of the solar system and the Moon is the nearest planet from the earth and influences human consciousness very strongly. That is why, although for each person on the earth there are seven zodiac signs according to his birth on the earth but the "Sun sign" and the "Moon sign" are considered more important. In western astrology, only the Sun sign is popular. But in Jyotish, the Moon sign is also considered more important because of the Moon's proximity to the earth and its strong influence on human consciousness.

HATHA yoga (a special branch of Yoga) understands the importance of the Sun and the Moon. Even the name of Hatha Yoga was created based on these two energies. Ha =Sun, Tha =Moon. Hatha yoga practitioners also knew that the seven lights (energies) of the seven planets control human destiny by controlling human ideas and emotions while corresponding with their consciousness but the Sun and the Moon are the most important out of these seven energies due to their strong influence on human consciousness. That is why, Hatha Yoga developed the Sun Salutation and Moon Salutation (a special series of Yoga postures) to please the consciousness of the Sun and the Moon. Hatha Yoga practitioners also use similar Mantra, during the time of Sun or Moon salutation, which are recommended by Jyotish to please the sun and moon energy (which I have mentioned earlier). The Sun salutation and the Moon salutation not only improve the destiny by removing the vibration of bad destiny but also give extra energy to our body and extra intelligence to our mind.

Sun Salutation

Just as all the seven planets of the universe exist in the human body in the Chakras in the form of light (which control human destiny), similarly the light of all planets exists on this earth also because the earth is also part of this solar system just like our body which I have already explained in the first chapter. There are different types of rocks on the earth which have been turned into many colors corresponding to the seven colors of the planets (Rainbow) by remaining in the earth for millions of years. The universal light (God) which turns into the seven colors of the seven planets, the same light turns into the seven different main rocks of seven colors. That is why the light of certain planets corresponds effectively with certain parts of the earth.

That is why, a particular rock on the earth is a natural storehouse of concentrated and frozen light of a particular planet. And these parts of the earth were called "Ratan" (Lucky Gemstones) by saints and were recommended to be worn by humans to increase the light (colors) of Chakras in the human body.

The cosmic light of which gemstone vibrates with which planet as known to the saints is given below:

Ruby	Sun
Pearl	Moon
Red Coral	Mars
Emerald	Mercury
Yellow Sapphire	Jupiter
Diamond	Venus
Blue Sapphire	Saturn

Two subsidiary Shadow planets...

Rahu	Hessonite
Ketu	Cat's eye

If someone has certain favourable planets weak according to his Janam-kundli, he should wear the corresponding lucky stone to increase the strength of the planet. We know that the rays of the sun individually cannot produce any effective result but if we use a magnifying glass which can absorb the same rays of sun in condensed way, then we can burn something by it. Similarly, a gemstone, when worn on human body, absorbs the cosmic radiation and color of a particular planet, and sends it to the relevant Chakra and improves the function of it.

The spiritual masters also recommended that if someone wants to get more powerful results from a gemstone, then before wearing the gemstone, it should be charged with "Mantra energy". As water becomes charged after repeating some words, each lucky stone can be charged with Mantra. That is why, before wearing a lucky stone, a Mantra connected with its planet, should be chanted.

By this way, the spiritual sound energy of the Mantra also becomes stored in the gemstone. This sound energy is understood by the sound of the Chakras. Any gemstone purified in such a way starts vibrating with an unbreakable spiritual energy. If someone touches or wears that particular gemstone, a subtle communication takes place between the color and sound of a particular planet and sound and color of the corresponding Chakra of that person. It is better if the gemstone touches the skin or there is no metal between the skin and the gemstone. This was the basis of ancient gemology which tells us how the light of stones can be used to improve Destiny.

"Wearer of Gemstones wearers the Luck"

528, Poorvarchik, Agneya , Sam Veda

Planets have their own favorite metals to vibrate with. That is why gemstones should be used with specific metals for more effect. But this is not strict rule. Gemstones should be worn connected with their respective day of week which corresponds with certain planet.

Before wearing the stone the first time, you can put that stone in a ring or a pendant into milk for a few minutes on the corresponding day of the gemstone of that particular planet (refer to the following chart).Then take it out, wash it with water, put it on your hand or put in the respective finger (read the chart) and chant the corresponding Mantra for that particular gemstone a minimum of 108 times. As there is place for seven planets in the Chakras, similarly there is place for each planet on the human hand and fingers. That is why, a certain finger is used. A pendant is also ok, if it is made in such a way that the light of the gemstone is in direct contact with skin.

Gemstone	Planet	Day	Finger	Metal	Mantra
Ruby	Sun	Sunday	Ring	Gold	Om Suryaye Nama
Pearl	Moon	Monday	Ring	Silver	Om Somaye Nama
Coral	Mars	Tuesday	Ring	Gold	Om Manglaye Nama
Emerald	Mercury	Wednesday	Small	Gold	Om Budhaye Nama
Yellow Sapphire	Jupiter	Thursday	Index	Gold	Om Gurve Nama

Diamond	Venus	Friday	Middle	Gold	Om Shukraye Nama
Blue Sapphire	Saturn	Saturday	Middle	Silver	Om Shanicharaye Nama
If needed~~~~					
Hessonite	Rahu	Saturday	Middle	Silver	Om Rahve Nama
Cat's Eye	Ketu	Thursday	Middle	Gold	Om Ketve Nama

Is Diamond for Love?

While explaining about the ancient wisdom of gemology, it will be incomplete without mentioning about the modern trend of wearing diamonds by women, especially in foreign countries, at the time of wedding or engagement. Have you ever thought how the mind of modern women picked up the idea that diamond is a symbol of permanent love and it is inevitable to wear at the time of the engagement?

If you want to know the whole story behind the diamond sale, please never forget to read a book "*Glitter & Greed, The Secret world of the Diamond Cartel*" by Janine Roberts. She opens the secret how it was planned to spread a rumor in society through big advertisements that giving diamonds to women is the most ancient tradition and all women must get diamonds from their men at the time of engagement.

If we go back to thousands of years of old Indian tradition, we know that the gemstones were worn (whether it was diamond or other gems) only after consulting Jyotish knowledge.

Although diamond is the gemstone of Venus, the consciousness of this planet is connected with beauty, love, arts etc but it does not mean that diamond is good for everyone. You can see that millions of marriages in the western world, where people consider diamond as a symbol of permanent love, are ending in divorce later even after wearing diamonds. There are several instances where the marriage ends in divorce within a few days or months. The most amazing thing is that almost all these marriages are decided by couples themselves after dating and understanding each other for many years because we know that no one believes in the system of arranged marriages in western countries.

That is why it is better to follow the ancient Vedic wisdom. Please understand that only those people whom diamonds suit according to their Janam kundali should wear them because gemstones are not just fashion jewelry. They have power to influence our luck, to some extent.

Light is Destiny.

Light is God.

(The *purpose of this chapter is to introduce ancient Vedic wisdom to modern educated Indians and foreigners. Lucky stones can be tried but as Lord Krishna said "Do your Karma first". That is why humans should not leave their Karma by depending 100% on lucky stones to change the Destiny*)

God as Sound and Destiny

You have already known that how much important Light is for human Destiny. There is a similar story about sound also. Before knowing, how sound can be used to improve human destiny, please understand the mysterious effects of sound on our life.

Science has been doing research on sound and scientists are surprised to know the influence of sound on every phenomenon of this world: humans, animals or plants. The most powerful influence of music is noticed on human mind because just by sound it is possible to make human consciousness flow in any direction. For example, when people go to a party and listen to some special dance-music, their body starts automatically moving and dancing. There is a kind of sound which, if you listen, can create romance in you. There is sound, if you listen it can create fear in you which is normally used in horror movies. By listening to that sound humans become frozen. There is sound when produced, gives courage to the mind, which is normally given to soldiers at the time of war, and you can become ready to fight. Similarly, there is sound, if it is produced, can take your mind to a meditative stage also.

Plants are also influenced by sound. If they listen to peaceful and classical music, they grow better. But if they listen to heavy metal, rock music etc they can wilt and die. Animals such as cows or buffaloes give more milk if they continue to listen to some nice rhythm. But the result is the opposite if they are exposed to heavy metal music. Even humans who listen to rock music or heavy metal music are more prone to become aggressive and negative than those who listen to peaceful classical music.

You can see the influence of sound on humans, animals and plants but all these sounds are external. The Eternal and basic sound (Anahad Naad- Unstruck sound) of this universe Aum which is the source of all internal seven Chakra sounds (Lam-Vam-Ram-Yam-Ham-Am-Silent Om) which are connected with human destiny. Although science is sure that sound can change many things for humans they it is not sure yet, how sound can influence even human destiny. But sound is God at the universal level and is Destiny at the individual level, when it functions differently in the Chakras of an individual based on his past Karmas.

Anahad Naad is the primary cause for the creation of the universe. But how does sound help creation? As there is an example from the experiments of Dr Masaru Emoto from Japan on water which shows that if we produce some sound, water starts turning into specific shapes of crystals, similarly when God by keeping some specific ideas in His mind starts vibrating Himself into Aum sound, the atoms also start turning into specific shapes and designs of the earth, planets, water, air, flowers, species etc and creation starts taking place in the universe, stage by stage.

Anyone who does meditation regularly can hear the internal body sounds. Ancient Yogis could hear the eternal sounds in their bodies in meditation. But the seven sounds are not the only sounds in the human body. There are many sub-sounds as well. Although science has not accepted the internal sounds of the body but from the interesting story which I am going to mention here, you will realize that now NASA is also coming closer to those internal sounds of the human body which Yogis had heard.

Although millions of meditation practitioners (who wanted enlightenment) from ancient history had heard those sounds within their bodies, almost all those Yogis continued their way to God (the source of all these sounds) to get enlightenment without giving much attention to these other sounds of the body. But there were some curious Yogis when they heard these sounds first time, they became very interested in these eternal sounds of the human body. The rhythm of those subtle sounds infatuated their mind. As much as, they went deeper into these sounds, they understood a very mysterious truth that not only these seven sounds (Lam, Vam, Ram, Yam, Ham, Am, Silent Om) are arising from the body, but there are many more subtler sounds which are arising from these Chakras.

They also knew one more interesting thing that the words which humans speak, whatever the language we use for communication outside, those sounds actually originate from these Chakras of the human body. They knew that actually "language" is already gifted in the Chakras by the universe to humans.

If you know about the theory of evolution, you may be aware that scientists are still trying to find out an answer to explain how a sophisticated language evolved only among the humans and not among the other species. Because evolving sophisticated language among only humans is impossible according to those fundamentals on which the evolution theory is based. Because if we think that language was developed by humans by themselves during the struggle to survive and to grow during the evolution of life on this earth, then why is it that other species, like elephants, camels, giraffes, rhinos, lions etc also could not evolve such a language. And, we know that each species has been struggling to develop itself on this earth. Without a sophisticated language, there is no chance for any development because humans are learning thousands of types of information through language which they also pass on from one generation to another through written script. They continue to enrich their knowledge from the experience of their ancestors.

We know that at the time of the beginning of life on our planet, circumstances were almost similar for all species of this earth. Then what is the mystery that only humans have such a language and other animals continued to grow physically bigger than even humans, sometimes even 100 times bigger (whales etc) than humans, but still they could not develop such a sophisticated language like that of humans? Even the chimpanzee, monkeys etc (which scientists consider as the ancestors of humans) their language is also less competent than that of small birds or other species. If really chimpanzees are our ancestors, then they should have at least a better language (better brain) than all other normal animals of the earth.

But when we look deeply at their communication skills, it seems worse than even those of small birds because many birds and insects show more intelligence than chimpanzees or monkeys. Even till now, monkeys or chimpanzees cannot be trained like dogs to help humans outside on road or to take blind people to the market. Chimpanzees cannot even make safe houses for their children to protect them from rain or other animals. But many other animals or birds have much better ideas to take care of their families or protect themselves when they are in jungles. If Chimpanzees were really our ancestors, at least they should have ruled all other animals of the jungles by their brain and language power and could have enjoyed a better level of life than all other animals in the jungle. But it did not happen.

The Yogis knew this simple mystery in meditation that humans did not evolve language along with the evolution of life on this earth. Actually language was already there in the layers of the Chakras for humans given by God under a cosmic plan. Those Yogis, who heard these sounds in their bodies, thought if already language is given to humans by the universe, then why should humans not pronounce EXACTLY the same sounds outside also for their communication, the sounds which are arising naturally from the Chakras of the human body? They thought if some language is made based on these sounds of the Chakras, then that language will be really amazing on the earth and humans can also speak that language effortlessly. Those Yogis, gave attention to these sounds of the Chakras and tried to separate each sound with its own unique and certain rhythm. When they were able to differentiate all sounds, they put those sounds into a script which was later called "Sanskrit" which literally means refined or pure. One such Yogi called Panini, who is known as the chief grammarian of Sanskrit, said that he did not make this language by himself, but actually it came from the universe or God. That is why, he gave name to these sounds of Sanskrit as "Shiva- Sutrani" (Sounds from Shiva=God).

Please look at the graphics below that show which types of sounds are emanating from the seven Chakras of the human body. You must have noticed some petals of flowers in each Chakra of human body. These petals actually symbolize what type of sounds are emanating from which Chakras in the human body.

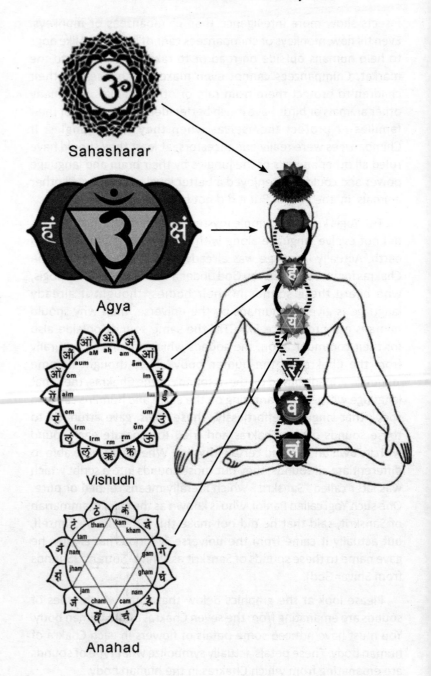

Sahasharar

Agya

Vishudh

Anahad

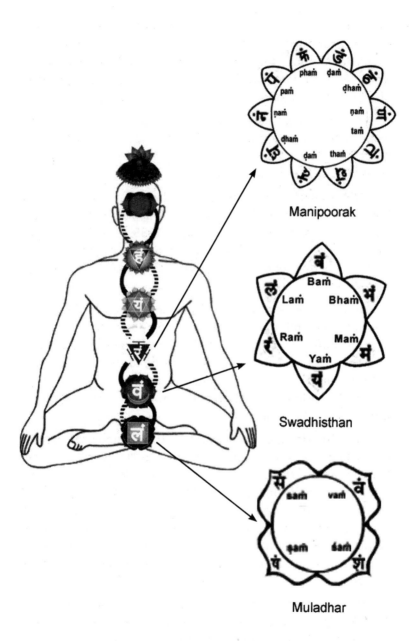

Manipoorak

Swadhisthan

Muladhar

That is why, it has been believed for thousands of years in India that "Sanskrit" is a divine language because it is based on celestial sounds of the universe. But how to believe that Sanskrit is a special language? Because there are more than 6000 languages in the world. In India itself, many languages have been recognized as official languages today.

A few years ago, a surprising thing happened in the scientific world. When scientists were studying the sounds, structure and fundamentals of all languages of this world, and when they came across Sanskrit, they were surprised to the core.

NASA researcher Rick Briggs devoted a big essay "NASA Sanskrit & Artificial Intelligence" for Sanskrit, which appeared in AI (Artificial Intelligence) magazine in the spring of 1985. He explained how Sanskrit is a totally rare and unique language among all other languages of the world. For him, it was totally impossible to believe that such a language can be developed by some humans.

Sanskrit is the best language for computer programming also. A lot of great spiritual literature was composed in Sanskrit and later many other European languages also originated from Sanskrit. Many people traveled to India. Some came to study Sanskrit and some came to study that ancient wisdom which was originally written in Sanskrit. Then all kinds of knowledge started spreading from India to the west.

Even after doing a long research on the unknown life of Jesus (13 to 30 years), foreign scholars like Nicolas Notovich and Holger Kerston came to this conclusion and wrote in detail in their books "The Unknown Life of Jesus" and "Jesus Lived in India" respectively that Jesus also, during the aforesaid unknown time of his life, traveled around the world and came to India to learn about spirituality like Buddhism and Yoga philosophy. The famous American historian, Will Durant writes in his book "*The Story of Civilization*" :

"India is the motherland of our race and Sanskrit is the mother of Indo-European languages. She (India) is the mother of our philosophy, of our mathematics, mother of ideals embodied in Christianity and mother of our democracy. Mother India is in many ways the mother of us all."

After knowing the spiritual story of Sanskrit, Madonna (the famous singer) also developed her interest in Sanskrit sounds. She came to India to learn Sanskrit. Later she composed a song "Ashtangi" in Sanskrit and sang it in her voice.

The sounds of our Chakras not only produce language but also they produce music. The music which you listen from the outside from some singer or musician, is first composed inside the rhythm of his chakras by putting these universal sounds of Chakra together. That is why, a musician is close to a Yogi from that point of view. The deeper a musician goes into his consciousness by meditation, the better he is able to derive more and more nice rhythms out of his Chakras. Because consciousness is a layer of seven Chakras, where all the sounds, colors and ideas are resting. If a musician does meditation regularly, he can perform well in music. Because meditation can take him deeper into his Chakras and the rhythms of Chakras start becoming clearer to him.

Sound as Mantra

Saints have been appreciating Sanskrit very much. They said that if someone speaks Sanskrit, he harmonizes his Chakras and mind naturally.

Just as we know that the sub sounds (Sanskrit) of the Chakras are connected with human communication, similarly the main seven sounds (Lam, Vam, Yam, Ram, Ham, Am, Silent Om) of the Chakras help to rotate the human destiny. Just as speaking Sanskrit words help to harmonize all chakras of the human body, similarly if someone chants the seven sounds of the Chakras (Beej Mantras), it can help his destiny. Because a sound connected with a certain Chakra, when chanted, spoken or heard becomes harmonized with the sound of the Chakra and improves the function of it.

If you have interest to improve your destiny in some special aspect of life, you can chant a certain sound connected with that Chakra. For example, if you want to deal with the arts but your destiny is not helping you enough, you can chant the sound Ham. Because Ham sound is connected with Vishudh Chakra which deals with the expression of our consciousness in art, love, music etc.

Knowing the deep connection and influence of sounds on human consciousness and destiny is a great help. The sound is called Mantra. See the meaning of Mantra.

Man =   Mind

Tra =   Freedom, Expansion

Mantra has that power which can save your mind from many problems and it can take you beyond the periphery of Karma and Destiny and can make your soul united with God.

All the seven sounds and sub- sounds mentioned before originate from the basic sound of the universe, Aum. That is why Aum is considered the best among all Mantras. By chanting this basic sound Ooo..mmm, you can balance and heal all your chakras and control your Destiny and proceed spiritually at a higher level because you are pronouncing that sound which has been already understood by the universe very well.

Aum is that vibration, which is flowing inside your body in Chakras also naturally and which is the foundation of the entire universe also. Once you continue to chant it, it starts flowing effortlessly in your body because our Chakras recognize this sound very well. There is no difference between God and the basic sound Aum of this universe. That is why Yoga-Sutra says:

"Aum symbolizes universal consciousness".

The Crown, the last Chakra (Sahasarhara) is connected with the basic universal sound, Aum. Almost all ancient Mantras were made from this Mantra.

Many ancient scriptures mention the power of Aum Mantra. Look at what "Mandookya Upanishad" says:

"He who chants Aum, is never destroyed".

The real meaning is that body is destroyed here on earth but such person's soul is never lost or destroyed.

Lord Krishna says about Aum:

"If someone says Aum while leaving his body at the time of death, he reaches Me"

But Krishna had also said that humans can remember only that thing at the end of their life which they have been thinking about or practising in their whole life. Mahatma Gandhi used to practise Mantra Yoga throughout his life. As he lay dying many people heard him utter the mantra (Hey Ram). That is why, it is good to practise the Mantra during our life, so that at the time of death also we can remember the Mantra. Because remembering the Mantra at the time of death opens the door to Moksha.

In ancient times (even now), in every temple, there was a bell near the main gate of the temple. When you ring that bell, the sound which comes from it was also Aum. Sahasarhara Chakra is also the main gate to the home of God, where Aum sound is vibrating. Some Buddhist monks use "Aum bowls" to create the Aum sound.

There is also another reason to chant Aum. Under natural laws, everything in this universe is indestructible. Things can change their shapes but nothing can be destroyed permanently in this universe. According to the same rule, sound is also indestructible. Whatever sound or words, humans speak on the earth are stored in the universe. They exist in the universe but cannot be heard, as sound exists in the music CD which we cannot hear until we use a CD player. Similarly, this universe is also full of sounds but we cannot hear them.

Aum is the only sound which has been chanted repeatedly trillions of times, with great devotion to God, by billions of Yogis, born at different times.

Such Yogis continued to chant Aum even after they had become enlightened to inspire others.

The basic Universal Aum and the Aum of spiritual practitioners have become harmonized in the universe. In future, if science is able to find any vibration in the universe, that will be Aum or it will be similar to Aum.

Some people think that if they cannot chant some Mantra with correct pronunciation, it is a sin. This is a big misconception.

You know already that Saint Balmiki who is well-known for his famous book "Ramayan", was an uneducated robber before turning into an enlightened saint and a writer. He was advised to chant the Mantra "Ram ...Ram". The literal meaning of "Ram" is the omnipresent God. But Balmiki started chanting it wrongly in the reverse "Mra ...Mra". The literal meaning of "Mra" is "dead". But because of his love for God, this Mantra also started working positively for Balmiki and made him enlightened too.

Even a small child cannot address his mother in proper language but still he is able to express his love to his mother. The Universe counts your attitude rather than your words. That is why, do not worry much about your pronunciation of the Mantra. A mantra can turn into something negative when it is chanted by keeping some wrong or revengeful attitude at heart.

There is another simple fact about Mantra. Any sound or word, if it is chanted thinking about God with love in your mind, it can turn into a Mantra. That is why, Mantra is not connected with any religion because any sound can work for you as a real Mantra as a protector to your destiny and give you enlightenment. In India there were many saints, like Ravidas, Kabir, Nanak and others who did not know anything or much about Sanskrit but reached Enlightenment only with love and devotion.

We know, normally humans are busy in their life and cannot sit at one place to think about or pray to God. That is why, if someone continues to chant Mantra anytime, anywhere orally or in his mind (even while traveling or cooking) it can help to make his destiny better. And, after death also, such person's soul moves through the world of subtle sound (NadBrahm). Each one is going to face the experience of death in life sooner or later. Mantra should be continued all the time in your mind, whenever and wherever your mind gets even a little free time, because time passed once never comes back to give you a chance to modify your mistakes. Those people who give a lot of time for Mantra Yoga, the basic sounds of the Chakras of their body become awakened and start vibrating more harmoniously with the cells of the body and with the sound of the universe.

As a few drops of water everyday can also fill a big pot over a period of time, similarly Mantra chanted even a few times everyday stores a lot of spiritual energy in the Chakras through many years.

And, with that force of Mantra in the Chakras, the soul is reborn in a good family in the next reincarnation (if someone cannot be enlightened in the present life), where it can get a favorable environment for spiritual progress earlier in life after birth.

George Harrison, John Lennon (Beatles Musical Group) never got that taste in their richness and international fame which they got from the experience with Mantra when they had reached India to quench their thirst for knowledge. You can read their experience with Mantra in their book "Chant and be Happy". George Harrison (Beatles) has said in one interview how once Mantra saved him from an aero plane crash.

It is easy to understand that if a Successful person like George Harrison also felt the need of Mantra in human life, then it will be a mistake if some people think that after achieving some success they will find permanent happiness. That is why, start your journey with Mantra as soon as possible in your life, before it becomes too late.

Mantra and Guru

We know that there are many books available in the market or libraries to understand any subject in the world, whether it is music, language, science etc but the universities still employ many professors because only books cannot help. Similarly, for spirituality only books are not useful, a Guru is needed. And, that Guru should be living at the moment. Because if we accept someone as a dance teacher who has died long back, he cannot teach us dance today. Similarly, a Guru should be living now.

The word "Guru" in Sanskrit has a special meaning. A Guru takes us from the world of darkness to the world of light (Knowledge). Normally people in our life (family and friends) continue to increase our material desires because all relationships are based on selfish desires. That is why you can see that even the most loving couples and family members also fight for their own desires. Sometimes even divorce takes place between loving couples and sometimes brothers also fight with each other for property. If this is the case, when person is still alive, then who is going to cry from heart when he dies on this earth? That is why, instead of becoming too much attached to this world, the Guru gives another meaning of life to soul to become enlightened, while living in this imperfect world.

Normally, in search of enjoyment, humans start neglecting even important things of life, if it is not repeated in front of them again and again. For example, even humans who deeply believe from their heart that there is God can't continue their search for Him passionately, in their busy social life. And 98% of the complicated structure of this world is full of Maya and it is there to keep you away from God.

That is why the human mind becomes like a free bull, which is very difficult to be controlled by any methods, carrot or stick. Only a Guru can control it.

All the relationships are with us until we have this body, but the guidance of a Guru not only helps to live peacefully on this earth but also helps the soul even after death. That is why, whenever some soul is selected by God, it does not meet God first, it meets the Guru first. That is why, after knowing the mysterious ways of God, some saints declared in excitement and joy that the Guru is greater than God.

Adi Shankra said;

"Guru Brahma Guru Vishnu

Guru Devo Maheshwara

Guru Sakshat Param Brahma

Tasmai Shri Gurave Namah"

Kabir said;

"Guru and God both are standing in front of me. Before whom should I prostrate?

I bow to Guru because He introduced God to me."

Siva Samhita says;

"Only the wisdom imparted by a guru, through his lips, is powerful and useful; otherwise it becomes fruitless, weak and very painful."

Just knowledge can be confusing for normal humans sometimes. Arjuna was an educated, intelligent person. But all his knowledge was going to be useless if Krishna was not there to take command of his soul.

God also wanted to teach the need of a Guru for humanity. God knows everything past, present and future and runs the whole universe , but when he is born into a human body, he also has a Guru to prove his humbleness. Lord Rama got Vasishtha as his Guru and Lord Krishna got Sandipani as his Guru.

Because God knows that He himself can't be on the earth everywhere in physical form with humans but some other pious souls can continue to spread his words until God is reborn again on earth to take full command.

Lord Krishna has said:

"For one who explains the supreme secret (Yoga) to the devotees, devotional service is guaranteed, and at the end he will come back to Me. There is no servant in this world more dear to Me than him".

And He has also said:

"And one who listens with faith and without envy becomes free from sinful reactions and attains to the planets where the pious dwell".

That is why, Guru spreads the word of God in a simple language to people who are willing to listen in this materialistic era. The Guru has a cosmic energy working around him always because of his personal spiritual practice. The Buddha had a big energy field which influenced people from far. But it was known to only those people who had already developed a soul from the spiritual practice of this life or previous life. When the Guru initiates a student into chanting Mantra, the soul of that person not only receives inspiration but also the spiritual energy of the teacher.

Mantra for Stress

As technology and life style are advancing , human stress is also increasing because of competitions in life. There are few people in the big cities now who can sleep peacefully without any stress.

Stress is just a negative communication with our mind. When you are stressed, if you check out your mind, you may be communicating negatively with yourself. Many people go on repenting about what they could not do or achieve in their life in the past or why they did this mistake or they go on worrying about what is going to happen in their life in future. Normally in stress, people continue to struggle with those negative experiences or thoughts which are connected with their Past or Future.

Such people instead of "planning" for the future continue to "worry" about the future. The simple secret of happiness is in knowing the fact that any kind of worry can't bring even a little positive change in any situation of our future event or past event in our life. If some change can be made, it is only with one's own Karma, plan or idea but not by the "worry". If you wasted two hours everyday just by repenting *"Why did it happen like this"? or "Why it did not happen like this"? or "What/why are they gossiping about me?" "Why am I not intelligent, attractive or rich?"* It means in one year, you wasted 730 hours plus some health as well as you may develop some complex which becomes a blockage later in your Chakras. Please understand that if you had invested those 730 hours in any important aspect of life without worrying about such small matters, you could have brought a big change in your life, just in one year. Success is just time management.

Even if, unfortunately, you are unable to invest your time in a good purpose, still you should never worry. Because if your loss is 20%, worry is going to raise it to 40%. Because worrying will affect your mind and you can't concentrate on the next plans and ideas which you need for your better tomorrow. That is why, to protect your 20% extra loss, you have to make your mind peaceful and energetic to keep it away from any worry even in the hardest of situations.

I have found that there are some people who become depressed if someone says just a few negative words and they cannot forget those words for a long time. People always expect that other people should always like them or appreciate them. Please remember that even persons like Socrates, Mahatma Gandhi and others could not have a perfect understanding with their wives or sons. The same is the story with many people great minds of this world. You can realize that when even these great persons having such great minds remained unsuccessful in establishing perfect understanding with everyone around them during their time, then we should be very clear that misunderstandings between human beings is a natural phenomenon. All humans still need a lot of time from their busy life to understand themselves, then how can you expect in such a situation that all people can understand you? That is why, you will find that a majority of the people on this earth have always been complaining that people don't understand them. Wife/husband says that husband/wife does not understand her/him. Son says that his parents don't understand him. Employee says, the boss does not understand him etc. You won't meet a single person on this earth, who says that everyone understands him.

Therefore, you have to keep you mind above such small problems of social life as a lotus keeps itself above the mud. All great musicians, scientists or spiritual seekers who later became pioneers in their respective fields had a unique trait of never worrying about what the whole world thinks, says or gossips about them. The criticism of the people could never divert their attention. Because, if mind continues to be disturbed by such everyday small things, then how can your mind concentrate on the great ideas of human life?

Mind is like a river and every negative thought is like a big stone to create ripples and divert its flow away from its main destination.

Mantra is your friend on the journey of your life. Whenever you feel disturbed and thoughts start disturbing you, put Mantra in place of your negative thoughts. Because when Mantra is chanted with deep breaths, your unnecessary negative thoughts and experiences of everyday, which continue to disturb your mind by floating in the blood of your brain, are replaced with good thoughts. When you repeatedly chant or listen to Ooo..mmm, it starts vibrating in the liquid of your brain and there is no space left for unnecessary thoughts. Mantra and slow breath help to make your mind more deep and peaceful. At the time of deep breath, if you say something to your mind repeatedly with force to change some bad habit or develop some new good habit which you need in your life, the mind accepts it immediately.

When someone has some physical ailment, he can easily realize that he needs a doctor or some solution. But when someone suffers from depression and stress, it is even more difficult to realize that the mind has a problem and the person continues to live in the same condition for months and years and slowly the situation becomes worse. Because from mind, stress spreads into the body and makes the body unhealthy because mind and body are not different. Body is like solid mind. If mind is like water, body is ice. Whatever is in the water, ice is made from that. When you start chanting Mantra and even dance for God, it is not only for the mind but it will help your body also because the universal sound starts spreading in every cell of your body.

The Dance for God

There are two types of dance. One dance is done as a profession and in that dance, the attention of the dancers is always on other people. Because this dance is done with an expectation of getting something from others either money or appreciation. That is why, in that dance, a person cannot be aware of his own soul. That dance is a performance. There is another type of dance which is not just performance. Here the performer doesn't worry whether someone is looking at him/her or not or whether someone likes the dance or not. In that dance, the dancer is aware of only himself/ herself and Nad Braham (the Sound God). Because in dance, sound plays the most effective role and music is the gross manifestation of the basic universal sound, Aum. Gross Mantra and Gross form of music help to awaken the subtle internal sound. You can try such a dance for God.

In such a trance dance, every moment of yours becomes a prayer and meditation. Such a dance releases all energy blocks from your Chakras. Your emotions can start erupting in such a dance as much as your consciousness becoming purified. Offer every feeling, crying, laughter, emotions, whatever comes out, to God.

After such a dance, if you like you can lie down. Feel your existence in this universe and on this earth, start taking deep, deeper and deepest breaths. Remain there as long as possible. You can chant Mantra mentally and meditate after this. You can bring your attention close to breath.

Mantra, Trance Dance and Dhyan can be a great remedy to improve health, consciousness and Destiny.

Sound is Destiny.

Sound is God.

God as Idea and Destiny

Have you ever thought that if you want success and happiness in life, how much an IDEA is important for you?

We know, to shape the history of the earth, Idea has always been a very powerful tool, although that idea was about life, radio, internet, aeroplane or anything else. Even people become successful in life not only just by hard work but mainly because of ideas.

I am going to mention the mysterious side of Ideas in this chapter and you will also know how a person can approach great ideas to change his life.

We know that an idea can be very useful in life, but the very important question is what Idea actually is, what is the origin of idea, in which part of the mind, does it live? Has it always been there inside the human mind already or does it live outside in the book or in the mind of some teacher which is revealed to us later?

Even if we believe that idea comes from a book or from a teacher, then how did the first idea come to the mind of a teacher or in the mind of the writer of some book ? If we believe that humans are born with ideas, then why do all people not have the same ideas? If we believe that we get ideas from our teacher or a book, then why do millions of people not have similar ideas, though the same book is read by many and the same teacher is met by many ? Then how some certain people approach the world with different and special ideas, while others do not?

Science does not know much about the mystery of ideas and where ideas live before entering the human mind.

How does it happen?

There is a big mystery behind the world of Ideas. Actually ideas are not connected only with books, teachers or events. They are connected with the universe. Ideas float in the universe everywhere. Because this whole Universe is the mind of God and Idea is the gross manifestation of God. We cannot realize idea in the universe until it jumps into our brain, just as we can not see any picture in the universe until it jumps onto the TV screen. Idea is an invisible thing but the whole world is ruled by ideas because all big changes happen on this earth because of ideas. Scientists can deny the existence of God because they cannot see Him. They cannot see idea also but can they deny the existence of Idea? No. Actually the existence of Idea proves the existence of God.

Basically all humans are able to receive ideas from the universe, but each one is limited to receive ideas differently from the universe based on his Destiny. As explained in the first-chapter, the universe is full of colors and sounds and each one gets them according to his own Destiny. Similarly this whole universe is full of ideas but each one receives those ideas according to his Destiny. Different ideas are floating in each different Chakra as different types of fishes live in different layers of the ocean, from top to bottom.

Although ideas are in the minds of all creatures of this world but all species (except humans) use ideas repeatedly just to live their normal lives. But ideas in the mind of humans become mysterious because of the law of Karma and Destiny. As light and sound function differently in each one's life based on his Destiny, same is the story with idea. Just as because of weak destiny, the colors and sounds of our Chakras become weak, similarly ideas also become weak in someone's life, if his destiny is not good.

That is why there are many people who do not have even a simple idea to get out of some normal problems of life, but there are some people who shake the whole world by their ideas. Therefore, Destiny also plays its important role to make someone a genius or to make someone ignorant.

Just as the strings of the sitar need to be played rhythmically to create a pleasing sound, similarly, the seven whirlpools of the chakras should be churned well under the influence of good

Destiny to catch good ideas from the universe by our consciousness.

Normally all seven Chakras function in a unified way to grasp ideas from the universe, but if we go to the details, we can say that certain Chakras are connected with certain Ideas in the universe.

From Chakra information mentioned before, you know already that which Chakra deals with which aspects of life and the weak ray of which planet can affect which part of your life. For example, if someone's third chakra is weak such persons can miss the ideas how to deal with society because it is connected with Jupiter. Their many attempts can fail to strike a balance with society. Same is the case with other Chakras also.

If someone does not have great destiny, he can be born in such situations where he cannot reach even the right kind of ideas. Most probably, he cannot get the right kind of book or meet a teacher, from where he will get some ideas to change his life. Secondly, if by chance, he reads some book or listens to a teacher, his weak Chakras don't allow him to understand the deep meaning behind any useful Idea. An idea repeated even hundreds of times in front of such persons, is never picked up by them.

Two college friends met each other after 15 years of gap. One had been very successful to achieve whatever he wanted in life and the other could not achieve whatever he had dreamed of.

The unsuccessful one was surprised at the great success of his friend.

"How could you become so successful?" he asked.

"It was simple."

"How ?"

"Do you remember a lecturer in our college days, one Mr. Singh?"

"Yes, I remember".

"He always told the students in the class, "Concentrate; concentration is the key to achieve anything".

"He used to repeat it every day in the class." The other friend laughed.

"The secret of my success is in this line only" The successful one said.

The same idea can be heard by many people, but if your Chakras are not functioning very well, you cannot pick up the power of some idea, even if it is repeated hundreds of times in front of you. That is why, by listening to certain ideas some people reached the pinnacle of success in their life. There are some others who listened to the same ideas but did not make any progress even after many years. The reason is peeling off all the layers from some idea and going deeper to understand its nuclear power is also based on an individual's own Destiny. We do not decide how we take some idea; our Destiny decides how we take some Idea. And, the importance of idea in the life of humans is so much that even a compensation of millions of dollars is not enough, compared to what they can lose by missing the right idea at the right time. Hard work of 10 years cannot take someone to that level where an idea can take him within one year, if used rightly.

Idea is Destiny

Destiny even plays a part in deciding what idea you will receive at what time. That is why if you find some idea at the age of 40, perhaps that same idea was clicked to someone when he was 30. That idea made someone successful at 30 and delayed your success by ten years.

Some people believe that hard work is the only key to success and anybody can achieve the heights of success by hard work. That is why many people who used to work 10 hours every day, start working 14 hours every day. Many years pass in that way. But after hard work of many years when they cannot reach there where their ideal successful man is, they become frustrated and feel hopeless. Then they start finding faults with themselves. A deep inferiority complex sets in them. During these years of hard work they could not enjoy their life, lost their health and could not become successful either. But if they go to the beginning of the success story of their ideal person, they will perhaps be surprised to find that it was not just only hard work, but was actually a special idea which brought this successful person to this level, where he is today. He got the idea to do something new or he got the idea to do the same thing differently which others could not realize. The credit of the big success of Bill Gates goes to the Idea of computer and Internet.

Some people say *"Ok, if people can't succeed by hard work only, they can be successful by a PLAN"*.

But without good destiny, you can never even realize that some plan is needed at some stage of life . Even to realize that *"a plan is needed"* is also under the control of destiny. Only those people whose destiny is good, can sit peacefully and plan, otherwise people never realize that a plan is needed and just run here and there frantically.

That is why, *WHO WILL PLAN AND WHO WILL NOT* is also under the control of destiny.

If someone wants to give good advice to someone that advice cannot be picked up by the person for whom it is meant , if his destiny is weak but it can be picked up by some other person who is standing close to him, if his destiny is good, just like an arrow that has been aimed at someone, but it hits some other person (standing nearby) by mistake.

Idea and the arrow move in the air and find their target under the control of Destiny.

When destiny is weak, even life changing ideas also seem totally opposite to the human mind. It is also possible that instead of understanding or respecting great ideas, you can laugh at them or violently oppose those ideas. History is full of such examples, when great ideas were ignored, laughed at or opposed.

The same thing happened with the ideas of Lord Krishna and the Buddha. The Ideas of Krishna were not understood by his cousin Sishupal and his maternal uncle Kamsa. Both were totally against Krishna.

The Ideas of the Buddha were also not understood by every one he met in his life. Two cousins of the Buddha (Ananda and

Devdatta) left their kingdom to join Buddha to get enlightenment. The teacher was the same for both. Ananda understood all the ideas of Buddha at last, put them into practice and became enlightened. The destiny of Devdatta was so weak that instead of trying to absorb the ideas of Buddha, he started plotting against Buddha. Devdatta forgot for what purpose (Enlightenment) he had left behind all his luxurious life, and he was going to lose that purpose.

But there were some incidences also when some people met Buddha only once in their whole life, sometimes on the road, when Buddha was walking from one village to another, and picked up his ideas, put them into practice and became enlightened.

In the western world also, even the Ideas of Socrates, Jesus and others were not understood by all contemporary people. Both were killed for their ideas. But some contemporary religious fanatics, instead of discussing the ideas with them, started opposing their Ideas. They thought they were doing a great thing by ordering to kill these people who they thought were spreading wrong ideas.

When such stories are read by the future generations how sometimes even great persons are misunderstood, and how foolish the contemporary authority was, they wonder why they could not understand the Ideas of such great masters. People born at any time on this earth always think that they are better informed and more intelligent than their parents or past generations. Therefore, people always think that if great people are born as their contemporaries or in their neighbourhood, they can easily recognize them and can understand their ideas and they will never be against them or in favor of killing them. But it is also their misconception. Because those people who had killed Socrates and Jesus, also thought that these people were trying to teach wrong ideas to society.

"Dark Age" and "Golden Age" don't exist in the history of the earth but they always exist in the Chakras of people according to their destiny. No matter, if they were born 5000 years before or will be born 5000 years later, they will absorb the ideas according to their own destiny.

Let us see what happened next after the death of Jesus.

1500 years passed. Until then, Religious authorities, who were teaching about Jesus and the Bible to normal people, thought they had understood all the ideas of Jesus and the Bible without any misunderstanding and now they could take care of what should be taught to normal people in society. A philosopher by name Bruno came up with new ideas about God, the universe and life. Bruno inspired people to think independently on the path of God without believing in any religion.

Top contemporary religious authorities could not digest his ideas and what he was teaching to people because his ideas became dangerous for the established religion. Bruno was kept in jail for 8 years. In these 8 years also, the Holy Office was trying to change his ideas forcibly. But Bruno, being a free thinker, was not ready to change his Ideas as there were not better ideas than his. Finally, he was burnt to death.

While burning Bruno, these religious people were thinking that those who killed Jesus were wrong but considered themselves great in killing this free minded philosopher.

There are many such stories in the western world. Once again, it was going to happen with Galileo also just 400 years later when he came forward with a new idea that the *"Earth revolves round the Sun"*. The religious authorities, who were studying, teaching the Bible, were not ready to digest this Idea also. A 68 year old man Galileo, whose Idea actually should have been respected or be awarded with national recognition had to stand in court like a criminal in front of the religious authorities to apologize for speaking this *"untruth"* to people. He apologized and escaped. He was kept in house arrest. But later it was proved that the earth revolves around the sun.

If understanding great spiritual ideas gives great benefit to an individual or to the whole humanity, similarly misunderstanding the right ideas also creates a big loss for an individual or for the whole society.

Ideas of many great free thinkers have always been misunderstood all the time and the distance between the humans and the Truth has been widened.

Although all types of ideas are useful for life but spiritual ideas have been very important for humans because of their deep impact on human life–because insects, animals are also doing similar things (eating, drinking, sleeping, making house, love, raising children etc), only spiritual ideas make humans different. That is why, people should be aware how much they need to be careful to know about spiritual ideas.

Although in each time in history, people have always been interested in meeting the real Guru, but without good Destiny, even if they sit and talk face to face with the Buddha, Krishna or Socrates, still they can't understand them. That is why, at the time of Krishna, the Buddha, Socrates and others, these great masters were considered just normal or "abnormal" persons by many people in their contemporary society. That is why, although many enlightened masters are born on the earth many people are never satisfied with any teacher and they continue to waste their life in doubts and suspicions without having any interest to search for the Truth sincerely.

The truth is that in good destiny, someone can be inspired by any Guru on this earth, but when destiny is weak, even if big masters like Krishna, the Buddha, Socrates, all together teach you face to face, they cannot bring even a slight change in your life, as we know it from history. That is why, the destiny in your Chakras decides whether you can recognize Krishna, Buddha or not.

Even Devdatta behaved like a monk and started his own separate religion. Many people believed Devdatta also instead of the Buddha and started following him. And Devdatta maintained friendship with king Ajatsatru also to maintain a higher and trustworthy standard than Buddha in front of normal people. On the other hand, Sishupal (cousin of Krishna) thought that a person, who wears clothes like those of a king, can't be special or God. He always felt jealous of Krishna and was not ready to accept him as a master. Most probably, Sishupal would have bowed down to some other contemporary saints or Yogis. Because it was a normal practice among the Kshtriyas to bow down to saints, Brahmins, Yogis etc. But he was not ready to consider Krishna as someone special or even just a normal good person and abused him in front of many. That is why, the conclusion is that only people with good destiny can recognize a real master and his ideas, others will try to judge everything from outside.

From the mind of the Guru, ideas start slipping into the mind of that truth seeker 's soul and that soul also starts searching for the meaning of life and finally finds it.

It is because of the power of great spiritual ideas that history remembers the names of Buddha, Krishna, Socrates and others. But history does not mention the names of its famous contemporary singers, actors or dancers. Because, ideas remain always as powerful and fresh, as they were thousands of years ago. A thousand year old idea can change the life of some persons even today, but a thousand year old music and dance can't bring any substantial change in someone's life today or entertain modern generations. That is why, the real existence of the Guru is not in his physical appearance but in his ideas. In simple words, we can say that a Krishna is an idea (Bhagvad-Gita), not a person.

Guru, as an idea, continues to help from far away and even after his physical death and even after your physical death as well.

Soul is on a Journey towards Perfection

Each soul is on a journey to perfection based on ideas. If you want to know how much your soul is developing and how much good destiny is in your Chakras, you can know by understanding the level of your ideas.

Science, based on Darwinian theory, believes that the body of each species is evolving on this earth. But actually it is not only the body but the mind of each species is also evolving and that growth is based on ideas. Let us go deeper into the story of the origin of ideas so that it will be easy to analyze your own ideas for the perfection of your soul.

When science goes to explore the mystery of the origin of life on this earth, it takes into consideration only the origin of the body, but it forgets to take into consideration the origin of an IDEA in that body for the first time. Science does not know how an idea clicked for the first time in the mind of the first specie of this universe, what was the physical condition or situation of that species at that time, who used the idea first in this universe, how it happened and at what time of the history of the earth it happened and what was that idea? In other words, science is not sure whether "body" and "mind" originated on this earth at the same time or at different times of history of life. Science is still missing that link in the theory of evolution.

For example, if we accept the amoeba as the first species, it is difficult to believe that the amoeba can continue its life without any idea in its mind. Because, without idea, why would BODY itself try to remain alive? Because the body of the amoeba did not know what it would get on this earth, if it kept itself alive. Because happiness, money, power, sex, all these did not exist at that time to enjoy which the amoeba had to keep itself alive. For the amoeba, life and death were the same.

What inspired it to live? Some idea.

From where did that idea come to that first body? From the universe.

Actually, which idea was moved in the body of the amoeba millions or billions of years ago on this earth and which ideas move in our brain at present, the source of all those ideas is the "Mind of the Universe" (God), where trillions of other ideas are also floating and from where ideas come to the minds of other all species. That is why, if scientists can trace the origin and history of the first Idea in this universe, they will trace God Himself. But they could not do it yet and they will most probably not be able to do it in future also.

The soul continues its journey towards evolution, step by step, from one reincarnation to the next reincarnation, from one species to another species based on ideas, until the soul starts reaching the idea of "Who Am I in this universe" and realizes at last that it is the "Universe" itself.

This journey of the soul in this universe is from the lowest ladder of consciousness (Atom) to the higher ladder of consciousness (humans) and then from higher level to the highest level of universal consciousness. Please see chart below.

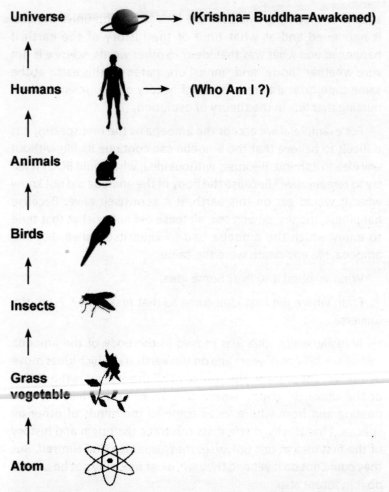

Universe → (Krishna= Buddha=Awakened)

Humans → (Who Am I ?)

Animals

Birds

Insects

Grass vogetable

Atom

When the soul is born in plants, it has more clear ideas than atom. When the soul is born in ants, it has more clear ideas than the plants. When the soul is born in the body of an insect, it has clearer ideas than the ideas of vegetables. When the soul is reborn in the bodies of birds, it has clearer ideas than insects and so on.

Step by step, the soul moves further to the bodies of other better ideas and at last it incarnates into the human body. In every next progressive stage of reincarnation, the soul has better and different types of ideas.

In the human body only, the real journey of the soul starts where the soul has the opportunity to think over "who am I".

The soul is reborn again and again in a human body until the soul reaches the idea of "who am I", because all other bodies before the human body are just to bring the soul to the human level. In the human body also, some souls reach "who am I" after a few reincarnations but some souls take many lives to reach this level based on their own choice.

Normally the soul is not reborn from the human world to the animal world, but those souls whose animal instincts are stronger than human instincts even in human body are born into the animal world again. For example, too much attachment to meat can take the soul to the body of some animal where the soul can enjoy its taste without worrying about the Law of Karma and Destiny. Or the soul can be born as a human in those islands where it totally depends on meat to live but it is a place where there is very little chance for self improvement and knowledge. After satisfying the animal instinct, the soul is reborn again in a better world to continue its spiritual progress.

"He is reborn here a worm, or as a butterfly, or as a fish, or as a bird, or as a lion, or as a snake, or as a tiger, or as a human, or as some other being in this or in that condition, according to his Karma, according to his knowledge" **(1.2)**

Kaushitaki Upanishad

God established this justified system to carry the soul step by step from the lowest level to the highest level (Atom to Humans) of consciousness, because God likes to give equal chance for all souls to grow at an equal level without any discrimination. If God makes some souls always worms (or goat, elephant, camel etc) and some of their "sister souls" always humans, it will be injustice to some souls who were worms, goat, elephant, camel etc and could not enjoy those innumerable opportunities which are only possible in the human body. The reason is, in the beginning of the universe, all souls maintained equal status before God and there was not any such situation which would make some souls favoured by God and some other souls less favoured. That is why all children of God deserve equal status.

Although a worm will not bother about remaining a worm forever in this creation, God however has to be careful about what is real justice with His creation. As in our human society, although small kids do not know what their real rights are and if a father sends one son to school to study and keeps the other at home, it is not justice with one child. But the father likes to treat his children equally and wants to give them equal opportunities for growth. Similarly, the universal father, God also cannot discriminate between any soul in this universe from the beginning by making some soul "worm" and some other soul "human" forever. That is why God had to choose this law of progressive reincarnations for all His souls for their equal evolution.

Although science could not find the deepest mystery of ideas, science is still trying to study the ideas in the minds of all species on which the behavior of all species is based so that the mystery of the origin of ideas can be understood. Science is amazed at the billions of new and unique ideas in the life of all species which they use to deal with their family, house, love, food etc. Science is confused by the fact why all these species do not just copy ideas from other insects for their survival which is a little easier, and why do they all go on developing their own unique ideas to live life on earth? Spiders, honeybees, scorpius, parrots, snakes, peacocks and millions of other species have special ideas to live their life which are no where used before, by any other creature of the earth. How do they get all these ideas in the first place?

A spider has an idea by which he creates a web and gets his food. From where and how, in the beginning of the life on this earth, did he develop this idea the first time? Actually, the spider should also have followed other insects, who were also surviving by getting their food in a normal style without creating any web, during the contemporary history of the spider.

A honeybee develops a sting in her body to protect her honey comb, which she has never seen anytime anywhere before, on this earth. If we believe that the honeybee learns this idea of sting from some other insect, then from where did that insect learn that idea the first time?

And when that insect or honeybee was developing that "sting" in its body, what were all other species doing at that time? Why couldn't they all get this idea? We know that millions of other species, having even a better mind, could not develop such a powerful weapon (stings or poisons) in their bodies to protect themselves and their children, although the main priority for each bird and animal is to protect own self and family, on this earth.

Some intelligent people say that developing a sting the first time, in the universe by some tiny brained insect is a more powerful idea than to create an atom bomb by a scientist. We know that how much deep calculation may be needed to develop the idea of an atom bomb. It means that an insect has that level of calculation in its mind or is it something else ?

Many four-legged animals finish making love in a few seconds, but why do dogs stick with the bodies of each other for a long time during the time of making love even having faces in opposite directions? They could also learn to make love just as many other four legged animals make and could produce children.

And we know that at the time of sticking with the bodies of each other, they could be killed or attacked by other animals even before they produce children because they can't run fast also, in that condition.

From where did they get the idea to make love the first time like this and why?

We know that humans got the idea from birds to fly but from where did the birds get the idea to fly?

Another important thing which makes scientists surprised is that why do all species, birds, animals and humans have ideas that they "belong" to others. In simple words, science does not know from where the idea of LOVE is born in species. If in life, everything is only for the BODY and PERSONAL SURVIVAL (as it is taught according to Darwinism), then why do many animals and humans risk their lives to protect their family, friends and even sometimes die for them? Why has love become important among the species?

Science is confused by thinking that even if sex was started just for reproduction in the universe and every species is living just for its personal body, then why does a man or woman fall in love with some other man or woman ? And in the absence of getting that certain person, sometimes commits suicide. We know that he/she can easily produce children from some other partner, because there are billions of men and women on the earth. But by committing suicide, he /she finishes his/her own body as well as did not produce children also. And, according to science, both things are unexplainable, "killing own body" and "not producing children". Because Darwin's theory considers mainly two things fundamentals that each species lives for its own survival, and sex among species exists just to produce children.

Now question before science is that the ideas of becoming the "fittest" and the "strongest" are acceptable among species but why and from where do the ideas of love and emotions enter the species?

Science does not know, what the source of all these ideas is. Is there some "Universal Source of Ideas" on which the behavior of millions of species of the earth is based? Do all species develop these ideas by themselves individually ? But it does not seem easy to create such great Ideas by animals or birds by themselves. Because if they are really good in developing such great ideas, why have all species stopped now developing better ideas for their life and why are they repeating only the same ideas since their life began on earth (as far as science knows their origin)?

Actually the ideas which the soul uses in the bodies from grass level to animal level are just to realize its own existence in the world and to deal with nature and the universe. But when soul grows to the human stage, a plan is needed for its growth. That is why, the soul is equipped with the freedom to develop many types of ideas and the Law of Karma and Destiny.

In our human society, the youngest children pass the kindergarten schools without going through any examination but when they grow up and move to higher classes they are introduced with a plan or exams. Similarly, in the universal plan also, from atom to animals all souls are free to deal with this plan without worrying about the definition of goodness and badness because of their limited approach to ideas. But an exam (the Law of Karma and Destiny) is needed for humans because humans know very well what they are doing and they are given a choice also. That is why if animals destroy all forests or do something wrong, they are not responsible for their Karma. But if humans destroy nature unnecessarily, they are creating some kind of bad Karma.

That is why, in the human body the journey of the soul starts to choose between the good and the bad.

And whatever the soul does in the human body is under examination by the universe, and therefore it is responsible for its Karma. If some soul misuses the freedom of ideas (because ideas should be used to do good) gifted by the universe in a particular reincarnation, its entry into the realm of great ideas may be restricted in next reincarnation. If someone helps others with his knowledge (ideas), his soul is born in those circumstances in the next reincarnations, where the soul gets a chance to learn more and gets more deep entry into the realm of great and better ideas which helps the person for the improvement of his own soul as well as for the progress of others.

But there are some souls, in the human body which cannot think beyond their own body, own house, own family, own lover. But these basic instincts, even small insects, birds or animals also possess. There are some souls in the human body, which grow to think differently in this universe. Such souls want to know the existence of everything around them, their own body, mind, family, lovers, flowers, mountains, oceans and the universe. Instead of falling in love with only its own body, lover, family or home, such souls fall in love with the whole universe. Although such souls become passionate to know the purpose of the existence of everything in this universe but it is not possible to do that because in this universe many mysterious things exist. And the most mysterious is her/his own self. That is why the real awakening starts in humans when someone starts thinking. "Who am I in this Universe". That is why this idea is considered the best in the human mind.

Until soul does know that it does not belong only to the body, family or home but to the universe (God) itself, the soul is never going to be satisfied or contented. That is why, the target of every soul according to Vedic wisdom is to know itself. And, ancient masters had known and taught that soul and God are the same.

But how is it that soul is also God ?

In the beginning, there was no one in this universe except God. It was the Universal Mind (God) which multiplied Himself and became many innumerable minds (All souls). The Vedic literature says that One became many.

Just as an ocean evaporates, and eventually becomes rain and falls down on the mountains in the form of billions of drops of water and all these drops again start their journey back to the ocean, and at last merge with the ocean, similarly, the universal mind (God) after turning into many individual minds (all of us) had started His journey back to Himself. That is why, as all drops in the journey are DROPS and at the end of this journey are OCEAN, similarly all souls during the journey are SOULS and at the end of this journey are GOD (universe).

When a drop reaches back to the ocean, it finds itself as an ocean. When any soul reaches back to its source, God, the soul becomes surprised by realizing *"Oh, I am the same"* or *"I am the universe"* or *"I am God"*. That is why, when you open the pages of the spiritual history of this world, you will find that many persons have declared like this in the highest state of their consciousness. The statements of many writers of Upanishads like "Ahm Brahmasmi" and of many other spiritual stars like Kabir, Sarmad, Mansoor, Bulleh Shah, Jesus and others prove this fact. Many of these spiritual stars, whose names are mentioned here, were threatened, attacked or killed by contemporary religious authorities by misunderstanding the practical experience of these mystics. Because religious group leaders who always knew spirituality theoretically considered the statements *"I am God"* or *"I am like God"* by such mystics as blasphemy or a threat to their position in the field of religion.

Whenever someone's soul becomes clear enough to state *"I am the Universe"*, the soul does not need other small ideas now.

At this stage, the soul goes beyond the realm of Karma and Destiny. As the drop feels complete in the ocean, similarly the soul feels complete only in God. That is why, even if you give everything, whatever is available on this earth, to the soul, the soul will still be missing and searching for something. You must have seen many people on the earth, even after having almost everything in their life are still restless and are searching for something because soul is divine and universal in itself. That is why every person feels deep inside that he is special and great. This feeling in the soul comes because the soul is a part of the universe, and not of the family or the earth. But people want to satisfy this great divine feeling from this world, from power, fame, body, family, and home. When they do not get that, they become depressed.

And as a drop, even after becoming one with the ocean can realize "I am the ocean" but still does not know what is happening at the other end of the ocean because the ocean is so vast, similarly, many Yogis or saints even after realizing "I am the universe" and becoming one with God, could not tell this world what the other ideas are in the mind of God or what God is doing exactly in other worlds of this universe or what the future plans of God are for this universe. That is why, although many enlightened persons could remember their past reincarnations, they still did not tell clearly to the world how the first time souls entered the universe. Because when someone's mind starts entering into the earliest reincarnations (animals, birds, insects etc) of his own soul on this earth, his memory starts becoming dimmer and dimmer. That is why, he can never reach at the point of the "beginning" of the journey of his soul in this universe. Even such enlightened soul also loses his interest to know the time and date of his separation from God in the beginning of the universe. He just enjoys the supreme peace by knowing that he and the universe (God) are the same. That is why many great saints remained totally silent on the question of God or on the question of the beginning of the universe or on the first entry of the soul into this universe. The Buddha also remained silent on such questions.

But by this well planned system, God keeps His top secrets from all His souls and at the same time reveals them to some extent. Millions of enlightened souls have been submerged in the universal ocean of God (and innumerable souls will be submerge in future) but still they can't explain through a simple formula to the whole world, what God actually is.

Those souls who do not want to reach the last idea "w h o a m I", continue to live under the law of Karma and Destiny. Not reaching the last idea "Who am I" means that such souls have to maintain their life only with those ideas which are on their Chakras and are gifted to them in this present life, based on their destiny from the Karma of past lives. It means they will always be in bondage of their own Karma. Good Karma will give them good life in future reincarnations and bad Karma will give them bad life in future reincarnations.

Now the question is, if some soul cannot reach the idea "who am I" and cannot have approach to better ideas of the Chakras in the present life because of weak destiny, how can they have a happy life? What is the recommendation, guideline or advice for such souls?

Sahasarhara Chakra is the place which is connected with universal mind, where universal ideas float at a higher frequency and slip down to other Chakras. If some soul turns its attention on the Seventh Chakra with surrender for universal mind, the soul can approach ideas. To turn your attention to this point, they called this process, Dhyan (Meditation). Dhyan is not only to get enlightenment but also it gives clearer ideas in the beginning stage.

Some people think it is focusing attention on the Third Eye (Ajna Chakra). But Ajna and Saharhara chakra are not physical points. In Dhyan they are the same.

Regular practice of Dhyan, can take any soul to the highest idea of the universe "Who am I" (Enlightenment) but it can show him other ideas also which are flowing at other layers of other Chakras which he could not catch earlier because of his weak destiny.

Dhyan is the easiest and natural process for the mind, if mind has not been trained to run after other things for many years. Normally when people are peaceful and are not suffering from unnecessarily stress or thoughts, their mind naturally starts going closer to Dhyan. If it does not happen naturally in someone's life,

Dhyan can be done with little efforts, anytime anywhere. It can be done even in the office during some free time or sitting close to nature. For effective and better results, a special and regular time should be fixed and the duration should be increased day by day.

The simple method for Dhyan is to relax yourself physically and mentally as much as as you can, sit peacefully (a chair can be used) or lie down, close your eyes, feel your own existence in this vast universe and on this earth, try to keep your attention on breath peacefully or on peace growing inside or on the part which is behind the two eye brows. Indian women put "Bindi" at this place. "Bindi" this word came from Bindu word. Bindu means a point, because this point is the highest point to develop human consciousness.

"Dhyan" does not mean that people have to practice Dhyan by sitting with a straight back in cross-legged position, as many people misunderstand. There are many other techniques developed by other Yogis. "Vigyan Bairav Tantra" an ancient book, mentions about 112 techniques of Dhyan which Yogis used to practice. You have to choose your own favorite one or a few techniques.

After practicing meditation for a few weeks or a few months on sahasarhara this point becomes active sooner or later depending on the spiritual practice of individuals from this life or from previous lives.

As a person, who has been lost in a dense jungle for many days, cannot understand where the right path is to go out of it until he looks at the whole jungle from the top of some mountain, similarly, people who are lost in the thick jungle of unsuccessful plans in their life, can't find the way out for happiness and success until they look at the whole jungle of their thoughts and ideas, from the mountain of Sahasarhara Chakra.

During the Dhyan on Sahasarhara Chakra, you will feel that you are standing on the mountain where you can look upwards into the sky clearly or look downwards clearly.

At Sahasarhara Chakra, you come into contact with the thoughts from two sides. If you look upwards, the universal mind exists at Saharahra Chakra and you can have contact with the universal subtler thoughts like "Who am I" or "What is this universe" "Why am I in the universe" etc. But you have the choice also to look downwards to look at ideas of family, success, love, house, society etc which are floating at the lower Chakras. All ideas start becoming clear to you which were never clear to you before, because of the weakness of Chakras. For example, if for someone, the third chakra (Manipoorak) is weak he can't strike a balance with society. Meditation for a few months will make it clear to him how he can make his role better in the society.

In modern human society, Dhyan is not very popular because there are many misconceptions about Dhyan. Many people think that meditation is only for the monks, not for the people who live in cities. Normal people think they are not concerned with God, they want only happiness and success. They think that it is not necessary to waste time on Dhyan with closed eyes when they can do some extra office work and get some extra money. But they forget that just as there is a connection between success and ideas, similarly there is a connection between Dhyan and ideas also.

Because success is just a small idea from trillions of other ideas from the mind of God. If someone takes a few steps towards God, he can meet hundreds of great ideas on the way, as Einstein met the theory of relativity when he was trying to know the mind of God.

Normally people think that Einstein was a scientist and his purpose of life was to think about science, that is why he could discover many great things about this universe. But there is one more secret about his mind. Look at what Einstein says.

"I want to know the thoughts of God; the rest are details"

Einstein was interested only in looking into the mind of God. The Theory of Relativity is just a detail, Atom bombs (which were made later from his knowledge with further research) are just details. His main aim was not to search for them. Whatever was found, it was just a chance. That is why he says that *"the rest are details"*. At the time of trying to look into the mind of God, Einstein could know many laws of the universe.

But in "Yoga sutra of Patanjali" it is written thousands of years before that Dharna (Concentration) and Dhyan (Meditation) are ways to know this universe at a deeper level. Actually the whole concept of Yoga is to reach the level of the universe. Dharna and Dhyan play an important part in that.

Before knowing what yoga sutra says about Dhyan, let us first see the definition of Yoga.

"Yoga is to stop the thought- waves from the mind".

Why does Yoga-sutra say so?

Because if many waves are rushing up and down in the ocean, can you see the reflection of the Moon clearly in the water on a full moon night? No. If waves of the ocean stand still, we can see the reflection of the beautiful moon on the water clearly. Similarly, if many unnecessary thoughts are running up and down in your mind, how will the ideas from the universal mind reflect on your individual mind?

First the mind should be peaceful and relaxed, so that the subtle ideas start reflecting in your mind which exist in the mind of the universe. That is the mystery how many saints by relaxing their minds and by going to Sahasarhara Chakra knew the mystery of Reincarnation, Karma and Destiny, Who am I etc.

"Yoga-Sutra" recommends eight limbs of Yoga. By following these steps you can reach the universal mind.

1. Yama   a. Ahimsa (Non-violence) b. Satya (Truth) c. Asteya (Non Stealing) d. Brahmacharya (Controlling senses) e. Aprigraha (non-collection)

2. Niyam   a. Sauch (Cleanliness) b. Santosh (contentment) c. Tap (Austerity) d. Swadyaya (Self-study) e. Ishwar-Parinidhan (Surrender to God)

3. Asana   (Physical Poses: this is popular now a days in many Yoga studios all around the world)

4. Pranayam (Breathing techniques to balance the mind and body)

5. Pratyahar (Withdrawal of all your senses from wasting energy on all external objects)

6. Dharna   (concentration) (In many scientists, musicians, artists and successful people this is strong)

7. Dhyan   (Meditation) (This is the next step to concentration. Yogis are here where they ask "who am I".)

8. Samadhi   (Immersion of individual Mind with the universal mind) (Samadhi is the answer to all questions and problems of life. Where the soul understands"I am the Universe" or "There is no difference between soul and God")

Anyone, who gives regular time to Asana (poses) and Pranayama (Breathing techniques), his mind starts learning to be standstill. He can improve his concentration and after a few months or years practice, he can be very deep into Dhyan also, where mind starts touching the Saharhara Chakra.

But we also know one thing more that there is very slight difference between Dharna and Dhayan in Yoga. Mind flowing towards a particular object, point or idea for a long time is called Dharna in Yoga. If we can extend the time period of Dharna, that becomes Dhyan.

Dharna and Dhyan are very close and almost the same thing in Yoga. The difference is only in time duration. That is why the great things which are accomplished by Dhyan, Dharna can also take us close to those things.

The mind of many scientists was moving in Dharna. And when Dharna becomes deeper, the mind can accidentally jump into Dhyan also. In that state of mind, we grasp different things about this universe which are difficult to be realized in normal minds. If people have discovered some thing or achieved something special in the history of our world, the secret was that their mind became closer to the mind of the universe. That is why they started understanding about this universe as something new.

One day, Newton was sitting in a park and an apple fell down in front of him. He paid attention to it with concentration. The mind of Newton continued to follow the same idea for many years "why the apple fell down towards the earth" and at last he could grasp the concept of gravitation. How was Newton able to do that? Was the mind of Newton in Dharna or Dhyan ?

Let us go deeper into the mystery of the mind of Newton.

Newton also belonged to the category of those people who think "who am I" and search the Truth of life. That is why, once Newton said;

"Plato is my friend, Aristotle is my friend, but my greatest friend is the Truth"

Newton mentions the names of two persons, Plato (the student of Socrates) and Aristotle (the student of Plato), because both these philosophers spent their whole life searching for the truth of this universe and life. But Newton did not mention the names of just only scientists. Because he knew that there are many people who choose science just as a profession, not out of passion to know the mystery of life. Newton thinks that his friends are only those who are searching for the Truth, not just only as a profession but out of genuine curiosity.

Newton was searching for the Truth of life but accidentally discovered gravitation, as Einstein was trying to know the mind of God, but accidentally found the theory of relativity etc. Newton was searching for truths from every direction. He is popular for his interest in Astrology also.

Actually gravitation had already been discovered by ancient Indian Yogis even many years before Newton which is mentioned in Surya Siddanta and other books also. But I have mentioned some names from the western world to tell you that modern generations can also understand how ancient Yoga knowledge has been helping the western world also in achievements. But west knows also how to use such knowledge and advertise it which India has missed. That is why, it will be sad if Indian generations do not learn to use things in practical ways from ancient knowledge.

Many world famous thinkers have acknowledged the contribution of ancient Indian sages to the whole world. Please read a few examples.

Albert Einstein said:

"We owe a lot to the Indians, who taught us how to count, without which no worthwhile scientific discovery could have been made"

Werner Heisenberg, Nobel prize winner, founder of Quantum Physics said:

"After the conversations about Indian philosophy, some of the ideas of Quantum Physics that had seemed so crazy suddenly made much more sense".

Arthur Schopenhauer (German Philosopher) said:

"In the whole world there is no study so beneficial and so elevating as that of the Upanishads. They are destined sooner or later to become the faith of the people."

Voltaire, a French philosopher said:

"Everything has come down to us from the banks of the Ganges, astronomy, astrology, metempsychosis, etc."... "It is very important to note that some 2,500 years ago at the least Pythagoras went from Samos to the Ganges to learn geometry.."

From these examples we come to know how developed the consciousness of Indian Yogis was whose minds were in contact with the universal mind.

In modern history also, the minds of Newton and Einstein were more spiritual than those of other scientists. From these examples, you can understand that Dharna and Dhyan are not only needed to achieve spiritual targets but also to make things better in our world.

Dhyan can help to understand the mystery of all types of ideas (ideas of happiness, success etc) and help to catch them which move in your different Chakras. Dhyan can also help you to learn to absorb those ideas, help you to control your destiny more effectively. But during the process of Dhyan, you will also understand that the universal mind (God) is like an ocean and ideas of success, achievements, relativity, gravitation, reincarnation etc are just like small pearls in that ocean. And the most valuable pearl is "*I am the Universe (God)*", and if you reach this idea soon, you have found the ultimate goal of human life. Because all other bodies and all other ideas only exist to bring your soul to reach this idea at last. Einstein and Newton were interested to know the mind of God or the Truth of this universe. That is why, their souls will also be born into those families where they can start their advanced journey in their next reincarnations soon.

You need a lot of contemplation to decide for which purpose you want to try Dhyan, like how much energy of your life you want to give for materialistic success by knowing great ideas and how much energy you want to give to "Who Am I".

If you are a student or young, it is also ok to try Dhyan to understand ideas and life more deeply to make a good life and to succeed in studies and work for the family and the country. Because our Vedic Rishis have not said that only Moksha (Enlightenment) is purusarth. They have said Dharma, Artha, Kama, Moksha, the four purusarthas make a complete life.

And if you are a mature and grown up person, it is better if you think "Who Am I" so that you don't have to repent later in life. Because those people who think about this idea, can be happy in all conditions of life and even can achieve the ultimate purpose of life (Moksha). But those people who never respect great ideas, even millions of dollars can't give them peace and happiness, when events happen against their wish in their life someday. Because life directed by shallow ideas scatters away soon and their mind falls into deep darkness, as we can see it happening even in the richest countries of the world.

What can be a worse place than a jail on earth for normal people of the world? But Mahatma Gandhi considered the jail as a tool to improve his personality and spirituality even more, whenever he was thrown into it by the British during his struggle for the freedom of the country. Some monks go to jungles in search of silence and solitude for the progress of their soul, but Mahatma Gandhi considered the jail as the best place for solitude and silence and continued his Dhyan. Gandhi had clear ideas which gave him a purpose of life, for which he gives credit to spiritual literature especially the book the "Bhagavat Gita" (which he used to carry always with him) to maintain the balance of his mind even in adverse situations.

If someone is trying Dhyan for the first time to reach great ideas, there is one thing to keep in mind. Dhyan gives many types of experiences. Dhyan shakes the whirlpools of Chakras and brings all ideas as well as memories to the surface of our mind, as silt from the bottom comes to the surface, when we disturb the water of the river. Because old memories are also resting in Chakras. That is why, at the time of absorbing great ideas, you have to deal with old memories also.

But why are there memories in Chakras?

We know that people like to do innumerable things in their life and have many plans and ideas but human life is short and time is also short. All things can't be accomplished in one life. And if people cannot put all their ideas into practice in one life, their Chakras continue to store those ideas to put them into practice in future. Such act creates the stage for the next life (reincarnation) to fulfill such desires. Someone sees a nice bungalow on the beach in this life, a strong desire arises in his mind to buy a home like that. But he does not have much money now and can't buy. But he says to himself "*I WILL buy*" or "*This is a MUST*". That idea slips down to his Chakras and starts resting there like a seed and waiting for the right time to sprout. Or on some other occasion, his co worker says something against him. He says to himself "I WILL take revenge at the proper time". But that proper time is not now. That idea also slipped down to your Chakras. All such ideas are resting in your Chakras waiting for an order to jump up at the proper time. Mind continues to store everything. Mind can't throw any idea, plan or desire out of it by itself, until you order it to throw it away consciously.

Everyone is carrying millions of plans in his Chakras. Some plans are from this life and some are from the past lives. As people make a storehouse in their homes to store many things in them because they don't know at which time, they will need what. Similar is the condition between our plans and Chakras. As people forget, how many things are in their storehouse even after keeping them there themselves, humans also don't know how many memories and ideas are there in their Chakras, although they had put them there themselves in this life or in some previous life.

When plans and ideas come to the surface of the mind through Dhyan, you will have to check whether you need them or you don't need them. You need to filter them because there are such negative ideas which humans have been carrying with them which stop further progress of life .For example, some people have been carrying painful heart breaking memories (of anger, hate, jealousy etc) with them for a long time. That is why such painful memories should be immediately thrown out from the Chakras.

When you start Dhyan, that idea will also come to the surface when you wanted to buy a big expensive house and you can also get some ideas how you can increase your income and buy that home. But you also have the choice to tell your mind that if you struggle to buy that house, perhaps it can take many valuable years of your life , which can be used to understand the meaning of life. Because after struggling for many years, even if you become able to buy that expensive house, for how many years will you be able to stay there? Because human life does not last for ever.

Anyhow, it is your choice how you deal with all the ideas which rise to the surface of your mind, whether you buy a very expensive home or not. But we should remember that human desires, ideas and plans are so many that they can never be fulfilled even in billions of lives. That is why, even if you buy a mansion on the beach, problems do not end there because when you go to the house of some celebrity or rich person, you will still feel poor by looking at his more affluent home or by looking at his more expensive car. If all problems of the rich or celebrities of this world are not solved yet, even after achieving many things, how can the problems of normal people end? That is why, be careful when you choose what is the best idea for your life.

Search, respect, and cherish those great ideas of the universe which can give you a special meaning of life because ideas can change human Destiny. Advanced ideas will make you think like God.

It was mentioned in the beginning that when destiny is good, people meet good ideas. This book contains those spiritual ideas that when some soul has spiritual progress from many past lives, then only the universe plans to introduce a soul to such ideas. That is why, spiritually inclined souls only , who are already decided by the universe, find and read such type of books.

When your ideas grow to the highest level, you will think for the whole humanity spontaneously, as our Rishis used to do and your heart will not pray only for yourself but for the whole planet. Such as;

"Sarve bhavantu sukhin, sarve santu niramaya |

Sarve bhadrani pashyantu, ma kashchit dukh bhagbhavet ||

May all be happy and healthy!

May all have well being!

May no one suffer from sorrow!

"Vasudaev Kutumbhkam"

"The Whole earth is family"

At this stage, you will be thinking just like God.

Idea is Destiny.

Idea is God.

Beyond Destiny

In Boudh Gaya, India, there is a tree. Prince Siddhartha (Buddha) had become enlightened under this tree. The night on which the consciousness of Siddhartha touched the state of enlightenment, the experience was so explosive that he started dancing in ecstasy constantly.

Although he belonged to a royal family he had never experienced this kind of experience in his life before. He could not control his spontaneous dance and he continued to dance almost the whole night. On that Full Moon night, people were sleeping in their homes with their families but Siddhartha was dancing constantly under that tree in the far away jungle, because he had broken the boundary of Karma and Destiny and a normal young prince Siddhartha had turned into "The Buddha".

When Siddhartha got enlightenment, he had two options, either to go back home, stay with his family and live the life of a king for the rest of his life or go into the world and spread the message about the purpose of human life and the secret of real happiness. Because normal people on this earth, without any spiritual practice, have always been thinking that princes, kings and rich people alone have real happiness, others don't have. But Buddha wanted to clear their misconception that the ultimate happiness of life does not rest in great kingdoms, palaces but there is another secret of real happiness for the humans which is not connected with material things but connected with the soul. He wanted to send his message to millions of people, so he did not go back home immediately but chose the second option of going to the people.

If a prince like Siddhartha, in spite of having all sources of happiness (a big kingdom, beautiful wife and lovely son) still thought, actually going beyond Destiny and getting enlightenment is the real way to happiness, perhaps we are making a big mistake if we are planning to get permanent happiness in this world.

For the last thousands of years, it was not made clear what is enlightenment. Even western minds could not grasp this idea. And another problem is that no enlightened person could make it clear to ordinary people because this experience is beyond words. There are many doubts and strange questions about it. Once someone asked me a similar questions during my stay in Australia for a Yoga seminar. The question was, is there any enlightenment ? If there is enlightenment, does it continue with the soul even after death? If it continues after death, then how long will the soul continue to live like this? one day, 100 years or.. ?

Humans ask this question about "one day" or "one year", because we think that "Time" exists. Because since people are born, they continue to see that everything is happening in time. They are born by time, grow by time, study by time, marry by time, and produce children by time, grow old by time and die by time. That is why, they are sure that "Time" exists and they start calculating everything according to time. But there is a mysterious story of "Time" also. Modern scientists are also arriving at another type of definition about the existence of "Time" in our universe.

In the world famous theory of Relativity, Albert Einstein explained the mystery of "Time" in a simple example so that even ordinary people and young can also understand.

"Put your hand on a hot stove and it seems like an hour. Sit with a pretty girl for an hour, and it seems like a minute, that is RELATIVITY."

According to this statement, "Time" has different existence for two different minds or two different aspects. For example, those people who are sleeping, are not conscious of any passage of time.

Those people who are awake, are conscious of time.

The experience of Timelessness in sleep makes the sleep enjoyable for everyone. Even billionaires like to go to bed to sleep whenever they get time. The poor and the rich feel the same in sleep. The poor forget their poverty and the rich forget their innumerable problems related to business and fear (of losing something) during sleep. When both wake up, again work starts. The rich go to office and the poor sit on the road to ask for money from people. But in sleep, both are the same. In sleep, five hours seem like one minute.

For God, one second or billions of years are the same. Enlightenment is also is a similar wonderful experience for the soul which is beyond the realization of "Time". The difference between sleep and enlightenment is that in sleep the soul does not remember whether it exists or not but in enlightenment the soul is aware of its universal existence and is not interested in anything else in the universe, like the mind of a drunkard who is not interested in what is happening around him.

Time exists for those souls which are not enlightened and it does not exist for those souls which attain enlightenment. The soul of the Buddha cannot feel that 2500 years have passed on the earth, after he has left his body. For the Soul of the Buddha, "Time" stands still.

God planned "Time" at that time when He had planned the universe of seven colors, seven sounds, and five elements to start the drama of Karma and Destiny in this universe. When people look at their wrist watches, they think "ohh.. I am late". They start running. God made "Time" to make humans, planets and the universe run. After making this universe run, God looks at this universe with a calm mind from outside , like a child that rotates a "Lattu" and watches it running.

Now science is also close to this conclusion that Time was not there when this universe began. And God and souls are actually before "Time" and this visible universe.

When some soul crosses the universe of Karma and Destiny of seven colors, seven sounds and five elements at the time of Enlightenment, it goes beyond the concept of "Time" also.

As much as, someone's soul starts moving close to God by meditation, love to God, Mantra, Yantra, etc, the soul starts understanding the mystery of seven Lights, seven Sounds, five elements. And 'Time" starts becoming clear to the soul. During this journey, many types of experiences start happening with consciousness. Many types of sounds and lights may appear as God is Nad-Braham and primordial light also. That is why, during meditation a devotee experiences Him in the form of sounds and lights of many varieties.

Nad Bindu Upnishad mentions:

"Being indifferent towards all things, after controlling his feelings, a Yogi with regular practice should focus his attention on Naad, which destroys the mind (thought process). By such practice of sound, a Yogi becomes deaf to all external sounds. After he crosses all obstacles (on the path to Yoga), he enters into"Turiya state" within fifteen days".

According to Vedanta philosophy, there are four states of mind.

1. Jagrat   -   Waking
2. Sawapan   -   Dreaming
3. Sushupati   -   Sleeping
4. Turiya   -   Samadhi or Nirvana stage

The purpose of all spiritual practices is to reach the Turiya state of mind.

As soon as, Karma starts becoming cleaned and love and passion of the devotee grows for God, he starts seeing the glimpse of subtle worlds. Sometimes there is no awareness of the body and the mind starts jumping beyond the realization of Time which varies from person to person how much time he takes to reach this stage, depending upon his practice in this or in previous lives. It happens soon if there is devotion to God and Guru. Each one goes through many such similar and different experiences. But the first experience with meditation which many people go through is that the soul understands that it is not only the physical body. The soul starts leaving behind the earth element and moves to the water element and understands it, because the brain is full of liquid (blood) and the body is also full of water. But in normal conditions, our consciousness is so gross that we can't realize that there is 70% liquid in our Body. Because whenever people look into the mirror, they see the reflection of their physical body in the mirror, but not of water inside their body.

rainbow pad
calepin arc-en-ciel

90
sheets
feuilles
4 in. x 6 in.

buffalo

With more spiritual practice the soul can reach to feel the fire also in the body, with which physical activities like digestion happen in our body. And when the soul come to the air element, the soul feels that it is floating in the air and it does not have any weight. (Some people misunderstand that your body will float in air. Actually in spirituality when we say that "You will get enlightened", it does not mean the body gets enlightened. Similarly, you will float in air means that you will find your mind floating in air, not the body).

When the soul moves further, it starts realizing that it is like space, which expands everywhere. But when someone continues to go more deep into meditation, he starts understanding that there is something more subtle than space and his soul moves further in the realm, subtler than space, in which even space is resting. In that stage, a person starts understanding that his real existence is not the physical body but it is beyond even all elements (Earth, water, fire, air, and space).

Consciousness starts enjoying some wonderful of experiences during this spiritual journey.

Normally by living for many years with this body in the world, the soul feels that this world is real and the other world is unreal but during its spiritual journey, the soul starts becoming more clear that actually this world is like a dream, and the other world is real. As at our physical level, we have a dream and we think that that dream is totally real but when we wake up from dreams, they have no value. Similarly once you go deeper into spiritual practice, this world starts looking like a dream. But without spiritual practices, the "soul" seems like a dream or strange but the material world seems real. That is the main cause of human suffering on this earth. Enlightenment is a stage when the mind can see this whole situation clearly from outside. That is why, each one of us should try to reach beyond destiny as soon as possible because we don't know how long human life is. Those people who are interested to know such another world, just a few months' regular practice of Mantra given by the Guru can give them the evidence of another world. When with a regular spiritual practice, once someone's soul reaches beyond the periphery of Karma and

Destiny, Good Karma will not give the soul rewards and bad Karma will not punish the soul and there is no desire connected with this world. That is why; there is no need for reincarnation of the soul on the earth.

Earlier we discussed that Karma and Desires from previous lives create the body for the next reincarnation and continue to maintain and run the body. According to this rule, a question arises that if someone becomes enlightened and all his Karma is finished, his body should also not survive because the body exists because of the force of Karma from past lives. Then why did Yogis continue to live even after finishing their Karma (or becoming enlightened)?

If you have been driving a bicycle for a long time, even if you stop peddling it, what happens? It runs for a little distance with that force, with which force, you have been running it for a long time and then at last it falls down. Similarly, people who get enlightenment, all their karma and desires are gone, but their body can run until the force of their past Karma (Prarabdha Karma) remains in the Chakras of their body, which had created their present body. If an enlightened person wants to finish that force also (go out of the clutches of present force of Karma) with his spiritual practice that is also possible. But almost all masters (enlightened) don't disturb that force which remains in the Chakras in their body and they continue to live on this earth as long as it runs, to help or guide others. Until they live, they tell others the mystery of life, whosoever believes them. When this force finishes, the body also perishes and they don't have any more force of Desire to create the next body. Because any good or bad Karma cannot create the next reincarnation by itself, if there is no more desire left to be fulfilled. Because desire is necessary for the soul to move further for the next reincarnation.

Some people are never interested in spirituality and they are busy doing other things in life but please understand that it does not mean that you are going to do something special or different. Because probably then you are going to repeat the same life story which other billions of people repeat on this earth and die at last.

Although each one thinks that he/she is special and his/her life story is unique and special but almost 99% people on the earth die after repeating similar type of life story on earth. Please check whether your life is the same as the next one or it is different.

When humans are children, only toys seem the most interesting things to them. When they grow up, they try to find solace and happiness in fashions, friends, sports or music and a feeling of romance is also born in them.

They like to wear different clothes than normal persons or want to color their hair differently or make tattoos differently or speak differently or behave differently by which they can get someone's attention and people can say "oh..ah" and they can feel that they are different from the crowd and their ego is a little satisfied.

They spend a long time in front of the mirror every day. If they can't attract a person they love because of some circumstance, they feel that their love is lost but if they become successful to get the person they want, still after some time that person starts to seem like a normal person or someone they don't love anymore. Then sometimes great efforts are made to get rid of him/her. Many stories of husband/wife fights or family fights in society also prove this fact.

Even love in life sometimes is not fully satisfied but now money, success and fame start attracting them. That is why they can't think anything about spirituality. If they get a little taste of success, they become egoistic and they want to make others envious because otherwise what is the meaning of success, if they can't look at others down from that platform of success on which they are standing now? But if they get the taste of failure, they become depressed. That is why it is difficult to tackle success or failure in life for those who have not trained their mind properly.

Age also continues to advance in this way.

One day, when they look into the mirror, they find that a wrinkle has appeared on their face which is telling them that the *sun of life*" is going to set soon but still many dreams, ideas in their life have not yet been fulfilled but some more desires have joined along with previous unfulfilled desires. One side of their inner voice says about the vulnerability of human life but another side of their inner voice tells them not to slow down the race of life. Because they think that if they slow down or give up the race of life now, other people will gossip or their rivals will laugh at them. The horse race of life continues.

Many more years pass like this and they find that they are very old now. As they were busy in the fast race in their life, similarly all their sons, grand children (if they had) are also joining the horse race of the society and no one gives much attention and time to them. They start feeling lonely even in this crowded world. Life continues to move further, and they become more old and sick. Now their body does not move, jump or work as they desire. Then, all those things, which once were very important to them, start losing their importance and they lose interest in everything. They are not interested in what their rivals are doing now, how much money their company is losing or making. They are just interested in keeping their body healthy, which continues to decline day by day. In fear of health, they contact doctors again and again. But time does not stop. And one day, they try to breathe but breath stops. The soul jumps out of the body and he/she is declared dead. Their body is consigned to fire or buried. The body turns into ashes and ashes turn into dust and dust also flies away in the air. No proof remains that they ever existed on the earth. People are forgotten soon after they die. Even in their own family, their great grand children do not remember their names. If family members cannot remember their name, why do neighbors or history need to remember their names ?

This is the story of 99% of the people on this earth and soon we are also going to be in the same list.

However, there are some who inspired by some strong ego, want to be a super star or celebrity, so that they can leave unforgettable memories in the minds of people. Because they are afraid to be forgotten by people or history. But in this universe, celebrities are also not exceptional.

Because just as we have forgotten the famous celebrities or stars who were born on this earth just 100 years ago, although they were a sensation among their contemporary people, similarly the famous celebrities and top stars of today will disappear soon in the dark fog of history of the earth just after 50 years or a little more.

Modern generations are not interested in a star or celebrity who was famous just 50 years ago. If you ask someone the name of the inventor of *TV* or *Phone* (although we use TV or Phone in our daily life) a large number of people have already forgotten their names. Because people are never interested in those people who are no more, although they are celebrities, famous stars or their own great grandparents. Celebrities and famous people of today can't be written in the memory of the people of the future forever. After a hundred years, many people won't even be able to remember that Bill Gates gave internet to the world because many other exciting things will happen in the world then. "Bill gates" - this name will last only for a few years in the memory of the people. "Bill Gates" name and his money will remain here but his Karma (If he can do some good Karma) will go with his soul.

"Name", "Fame" and "money" are connected with the body, not with the soul. Because soul is on a journey, not the body. The body will be destroyed after a few years and the soul will continue its next journey by carrying the force of Karma with it, after leaving behind name, fame, money, family of the present life. That is why we should never forget the main purpose of human life in the excitement of contemporary circumstances or problems of our life, in which we are flowing now. Because such types of circumstances and problems were also faced by billions of people born before us on this earth and they had also died without solving all problems of their life and without leaving any permanent mark in the history of this earth and without getting enlightenment also. That is why our body, name, fame, money, education should be used for the progress of our soul and of others also.

A small bug which is born during the rains survives only for one week on this earth. Humans can feel pity that how small a life it has. What can anyone achieve in such a short life ? But the sense of time to the bug is given in such a way by nature that he does never realize that one week is short time. During this one week, he makes his own home, fights for his own territory, falls in love, produces children and takes care of them. In this small life, he has his own rivals also.

If we look from the universe, the 70 to 80 years of time of human life in the history of billions of years of this earth, is also equal to one second of time on our wrist watch. Even there are trees which live for thousands of years. But humans have no sense of time. But they have time to waste in life.

Intelligent people should remember that each one has to go through this life cycle. And those people who will not be much influenced by every stage of their life and become "Sthit-Pragya"(Man of balanced intellect) they become great persons and find the highest purpose of life, enlightenment.

Interest in spirituality should be established among younger people from a young age. Because passion to search something at a young age is stronger, although that passion is to search about success or love or enlightenment. That is why many great masters were enlightened when they were in their thirties. During the younger years, Prince Siddhartha was also very sensitive and passionate. The passion of his life once inspired him to win that *"Warrior competition"* (a culture among warrior class people in ancient India) to get the most beautiful woman, Yashodara, which was arranged to find a suitable match for Yashodara. The same passion and enthusiasm of Siddhartha's life, again did not allow him to rest before reaching the ultimate purpose of human life, Nirvana. With enthusiasm and passion, Siddhartha could get both in his life, the most desirable woman and the most desirable aim of life, Enlightenment. But because of lack of enthusiasm and passion in life, many people could not achieve their any purpose. Their plans remained only plans. That is why just remember one thing that enthusiasm and passion are the secrets for all material, scientific or spiritual achievements of this life. For example, people think that Einstein must have had some special talent, therefore, he must have done such wonders with his brain and we can't be like him. But please, look at what he says.

"I have no special gift - I am only passionately curious"

Passion is the key to all achievements in life. Siddhartha (Buddha) had become 50% enlightened on that day when he had passionately contemplated on the bitter truths of human life, sickness, old age and death, and the other 50%, he finished by practice. Normal people find it difficult to practice spirituality because they don't have the time to think over sickness, old age and death. They know sickness, when sickness comes to them. They know old age, when they are already old. They know death when death comes and sits on their bed . At that time, it is too late and they can't prepare for anything. The only secret of success of Siddhartha in Enlightenment and other million saints is that those great persons could think and calculate on things before these events could happen in their life.

To inspire the mind towards spirituality, everyone should study and think about the life and thoughts of great saints and he should also spend some time alone in a silent place away from the crowd regularly in a contemplating mood to understand the deep meaning of great thoughts. Because great thoughts help even in the worst situations of life.

That is why to develop passion for God is to know as much as you can know about God. Because the more you know, more you want to know. The less you know, the less you want to know. Try Mantra, Yantra, Tantra, Dhyan, Dance for God etc whatever you like to take your consciousness to highest stage. But if these methods are not enough to continue your spiritual journey, there are many more.

"VigyanBairavTantra" (Shiva speaks to Shakti when she asks about the secrets of the universe, life and how to get enlightenment) offers 112 techniques of meditation. Tantra is a spiritual science like Mantra, Yantra etc but because of misunderstanding created by some people, Tantra became a less popular word as compared to Mantra and Yantra. We know that Mantra and Yagya were also used in ancient time by some people to destroy the enemy or get some negative power but it does not mean that Mantra or Yagya are bad. Similarly, Tantra has many uses and good people like to use it for a great purpose. Tantra means "expansion" of consciousness. Tantra techniques were used to expand the consciousness (which is limited in body now) for enlightenment to understand the mystery of life, universe and God through every experience of body (like seeing, smelling, touching etc) in deep conscious meditative way. Humans live a normal life and experience many things everyday. As Krishna said to Arjuna if someone, while even engaged in war or everyday activities, performs his duty without putting his personal ego in it, he is moving towards Enlightenment, similarly, Shiva also states that all experiences which happen in our day to day life can open our experiences to God. Even looking at the moon can be meditation, even dancing can be meditation, love can be meditation. And when someone understands the source of all these senses (SIGHT, HEARING, TASTE, SMELL etc) which are happening in our body from the spiritual point of view, he can jump beyond the law of Karma and Destiny. Because these senses exist in this universe, because there is a cosmic source and God is functioning behind them. Without God, these experiences can't exist at all even at our physical level and the material world. Let us see how you can understand your senses in their most mysterious spiritual sense, by which you start your spiritual journey.

Science has always been busy trying to open the mystery of this universe from all external mysterious phenomena, whether it is atom, light, sound, air, water, planets, galaxies. That is why, science developed many instruments with which, it can look outside, at this universe. But Tantra goes the way round. According to Tantra, in this universe, only atom, air, fire, water, sun or flowers exist, we also exist. Our body also exists. If the universe is a miracle or mystery for science, for Tantra the first miracle is our own self, our own body, our own experience. Whatever experience we are facing through our body, although it is taste, smell, sight, hearing, breath or sex, is also the biggest miracle of this universe. That is why, to know the mystery of this universe, there is no need to look into the universe by turning head upwards. The first steps should be taken from our own selves. Because nothing can be more close to us than our own body and its experiences.

We experience many things through our body. If someone can learn how to use the functions and experiences of his body in Tantra way, he is not far from spiritual progress. According to Tantra, there are three types of uses of all our senses (eyes, ears, tongue etc) of our body. The first use is the necessary use of some sense (animals also know this use) and the second use is to enjoy the full use of that sense (normally humans do that). The third use is realizing the reflection of God in that sense (Tantra Yogis do that). For example, an eye can be used in three ways, to see by it (animals also do that), to enjoy beauty or learn something by it (Humans do it) and to know the mystery of God from the existence of mysterious power of "sight" in our universe (Tantra Yogis do that).

Let us take one example to understand it in depth. When you look at something, the sky, the moon, the vast ocean etc, sometimes you are amazed at the wonderful existence of such things in our universe and we say "*wow, it is wonderful*". But these words come for the ocean or the moon or the flower but not for your own eye. Because eyes are with you always. You are born with them. You don't feel any miracle within your eyes. But miracle exists in our eyes, and to know that miracle scientists have tried for years but the answer has not been found yet. And the miracle of our eyes is so big that if you say hundreds of times "Wow …Wow" each morning when you get up from bed and open your eyes, still it is not enough. But humans don't say it even once in their whole life.

To understand, how big a miracle "sight" is, once some scientists had taken some born-blind children to some isolated island where the children did not have any chance to realize that "sight" exists at all in the human body. The scientists who lived with them there, to take care of the children, also behaved just like born-blinds. There was no chance left for the children to feel the idea of sight in human life. Even when those children grew up and became adults, no one of them ever showed any restlessness or incompleteness in their body without eyes. They started living with their bodies naturally. Instead of complaining about the absence of something in their bodies, they developed other alternatives to make their life more comfortable without eyes, for example, by trying to listen to sound more clearly coming from every direction and by developing the sense of touch more effectively. But they never complained that they were missing some special power in their body. And whenever they felt some danger they did not want to "see" which type or shape of danger was coming but they wanted to feel it by hearing the sound more clearly to realize, from which side the danger was coming, so that they could find their way to safety.

Now the question before the scientists was and is that even after having highly developed minds, humans can't even imagine that they need "sight" in their bodies, then how millions of years ago, some tiny insects of our earth thought that they needed sight, if we believe in Darwin theory. Even if somehow they realized that they needed something like SIGHT in their bodies, how could they develop such a great power by themselves?

We are discussing those eyes, with which you are reading this book now. And with which eyes, you look at the sky, the moon and the sun everyday and watch TV. Why is eye sight planned for us in the universe? Did you ever get time from your busy schedule to think on this issue?

"Sight" is not the question of modern science, because modern science is born recently. Thousands of years ago also, Yogis calculated such matters and reached a simple conclusion by going into the depth of their meditation that sight is not something else in our world but God manifesting Himself through the eyes of species on this earth. That is why, Tantra says that God can be realized even from "sight". Read the line from an ancient scripture *Kena Upanishad.*

"That (God) which cannot be seen by the eyes, because by whom the eyes see"

Read what a verse of *"Vigyan BairavTantra"* says...

"Be aware, YOU are,

With sweet of touch,

When singing, SEEING, tasting,

and discover the Ever living (Soul and God)" .

Tantra teaches that when you look at something, look consciously. When you become surprised at the beauty of the full moon, you should learn to be surprised about the miracle of your eye also. If someday you understand which force is looking out from your eyes, you start understanding the entire existing cosmic function.

You can try similar Tantra experiment with other senses also. For example, if you want to experiment with the nose, take some flowers in your hand and continue to smell it with a gap of a few seconds or minutes. When you smell the flower, just try to be conscious who is realizing this smell inside your body, the nose or someone else. If not the skin of the nose, then who is this "someone else"? That "someone else" (soul) is the destination of all spiritual scriptures and practices.

Ears are used only to listen to sound in the world. Animals also experience sound with their ears. But humans go further and can use sound (Music) for pleasure. But Tantra inspires further to realize this *"divine hearing force"* which is working in our ears.

Tantra says, all these senses have spiritual background which connect physical life of humans   back to the spiritual world of God.

Scientists are unable to understand, *WHY* and *HOW* powers like sight, hearing, smelling, sexuality etc jumped into the universe with the plan of life in the first place, because life was 100% possible to -originate and continue even without eyes, ears, taste and sex on this earth.

Why do these miraculous forces exist in the universe and in our bodies?

Billions of humans take birth with these miracles, live in miracles and at last die in miracles but never realize that any miracle exists at all. In each of these miracles, God is manifesting Himself very clearly but people are unaware of this fact. For some people, there is nothing like God or miracle but for some people each blade of grass or each drop of rain falling from sky is also a miracle. That is why, Einstein said:

"There are two ways to live this life, everything is miracle and nothing is miracle".

The reason why Einstein became such a genius personality of the world is because he was able to see the miracle all around him in this universe, which he was trying to understand by his skeptic mind. When someone tries to solve such miracles through rational mind, he becomes a scientist and when someone tries to solve the miracle by love and trust, he becomes a devotee or Yogi. That is why, humans need to wake up from that deep sleep which society and everyday routine work for many years gave us and we became a machine and forgot every miracle of human life on this earth. When normal people want to see miracles and to get some excitement, they read some mystery or suspense stories or go to magic shows because they are searching for some miracle somewhere outside. Miracle gives humans excitement but they remain unaware of those all shocking miracles, they are living with their whole life on earth. If someone realizes the real miracle of his own self, the imaginative stories can't entertain him anymore, just as cat and rat stories don't entertain an adult person.

A man went to Siddhartha and asked him.

"Are you God?"

"No" Siddhartha replied.

"Are you Messiah?"

"No"

"Then, who are you?"

"Buddha"

"Buddha" is a Sanskrit term, which means "Awakened". Later Siddhartha became famous by this name.

Why does Siddhartha say, he is awakened?

Does he mean that other people are sleeping?

Yes.

He just wanted to say that he has awakened to the deep truths of life, over which people are sleeping.

Siddhartha spent his whole life giving the same message of "wake up" to people. When Buddha says "wake up" to people, people think, why is this man telling them to wake up because they are not sleeping, they are already awake, they are going to office, earning good money, going to parties, running their families. More than 2500 years have passed but still people don't know what "Awakening" Buddha was talking about. Because people can't see that what Buddha can see and billions of people have been taking birth and dying in a "*sleeping*" state of their mind on this earth.

Each one is complaining about something, work, business, parents, children, wife, boss, friends etc. But there are a few who have the time to think why Buddha is saying that people are sleeping.

Although many enlightened persons are born on the earth and many great scriptures are available on the earth in the last thousands of years, but they have not been able to make all the people of the earth enlightened. Because if in some city, all are born blind and someone comes there with eyes and tells them that they are blind, they cannot even believe it. Because they want to confirm it from their other friends who are also blind. All the blind people, after a long discussion with each other, reach this conclusion that they themselves are normal but the other person is abnormal and strange. They feel safe with other blind people, but don't feel safe with a single person who can see. That is why the words of Krishna, Buddha and others are only for a few, others feel safe with blind crowds.

Searching for God in temples is good but the real temple of God is our own body. That is why if you cannot visit a temple, sit anywhere or close to a Guru, close your eyes, surrender your heart to God.

Start your journey to God soon. He is waiting for you sitting at the doorstep (Sahasarhara Chakra) as a mother sits and waits at the doorstep when her child does not return home soon from school or play.

Dance, sing, pray, be a vegetarian and know the Truth. Life is short and it is not to be wasted.

Shanti Shanti Shanti..

* *Become member of YOGAJYOTI to keep in touch with YOGAJYOTI activities, by sending email to enquiry@yogajyoti.com*
* *Arrange YOGAJYOTI camp/Seminar in your city.*
* *Help (Mentally, physically, financially etc) to spread this ancient YOGA wisdom to those souls, who are suffering in life without any light or hope.*